Con

CW01501867

STANDING FREE

STANDING FREE

The Life and Times of
THEO TEN CAAT

With Nick Brown

First published by Pitch Publishing, 2025

Pitch Publishing
9 Donnington Park,
85 Birdham Road,
Chichester, West Sussex,
PO20 7AJ
www.pitchpublishing.co.uk
info@pitchpublishing.co.uk

A CIP catalogue record is available for this book
from the British Library.

ISBN 978 1 80150 945 9

Printed and bound on FSC® certified paper in line with
our continuing commitment to ethical business practices,
sustainability and the environment.

Typesetting and origination by Pitch Publishing
Printed and bound in India by Thomson Press India Ltd.

Foreword by Robert Connor

THEO TEN Caat was the fifth Dutch signing during Alex Smith's tenure at Aberdeen.

Another Theo, Theo Snelders, had been an outstanding signing to replace the legendary goalkeeper Jim Leighton, and Hans Gillhaus must have been up there with the best strikers ever to pull on a Dons shirt. Big front man Willem van der Ark and defensive midfielder Peter van de Ven did not make such a big impact but were still high-quality players and very good additions to the squad that gave the management team options in different games.

Theo was the last of the Dutchmen to arrive at the club and, being left-sided, was the one I would be in most contact with on the pitch. Although predominant left-footed, Theo was a very well-balanced player and strong on his right side, too. He was what we would think of in Scotland as a typical European midfielder with his high technical skill and great game awareness.

I remember him arriving for training on his first day with a big smile on his face. That wasn't just by way of introduction to us, he always had that, and he also wore some pretty bright-coloured clothes. He always had them too! He wasn't much of a fashion icon, if truth be told, but he was a really talented player and was also a deep thinker on the game, and I wasn't surprised to see he went on to have a successful career with his own coaching school after his playing days.

Sadly, Theo didn't enjoy the best of times at Pittodrie and we did not see the best of him. Alex Smith was sacked not long after Theo arrived, which naturally affected him, but I think what was a bigger hurdle for Theo to overcome was the British style of football. He was brought up with a different mindset in Holland, where they had been developing 'Total Football' since the golden days of Rinus Michels and Johan Cruyff in the 1970s. At the same time, I think the Europeans were also trying to minimise the physical style of play, which is what we had in the UK, by modifying the rules to allow the more skilful players to operate without fear of flying tackles or tackles from behind.

I experienced the results of that as, by the time Theo arrived at the club in 1991, I had been at Pittodrie for five years and had played against quite a few European sides. My everlasting memory of those games is that I always thought the other side had 15 or 16 players on the pitch. They always had far more possession of the ball, and most of the time it felt like we were chasing shadows. During those matches we were forever complaining to the referee for giving fouls against us that would never have been given by a Scottish referee. When you look at the style of play in the English top flight today, and the number of foreign coaches and players that it's taken to establish that, I am certain that is the culmination of the European 'revolution' in the 70s and 80s.

The Europeans were way ahead of us in that respect, and I think Theo was unlucky to be in Scotland during that transitionary period when we were still playing the traditional British style of football and he had something completely different to the rest of us in his head. I could see it was incredibly frustrating for him and, although he was a very laid-back and happy-go-lucky guy, Theo was incredibly serious about his football and he was not slow to give his opinion on things that he felt were not going right. There were many occasions where Theo would offer an alternative opinion to what we were being asked to do in training or in matches but, when all was said and done, everything would be left on the training pitch and he would put his colourful gear back on and walk out the door with that big smile on his face.

Theo was a great character to have around the club.

Robert Connor, 2024

Introduction

'SMITH PURRS Over Top Caat'. Let's be honest, it was a headline writer's dream when Aberdeen manager Alex Smith signed Theo ten Caat from FC Groningen in 1991. Come on, how many puns can you think of?

A skilful attacking left-footed playmaker with an eye for goal was exactly what the team needed at the time. Aberdeen supporters will know some of the story of what happened during his period at the club, but here Theo gives an eye-opening account in his own words of his time in Scotland, not only on the pitch but behind the scenes as well.

I first spoke with Theo when researching my book, *Going Dutch*, the story of how and why the Dons had a cluster of players from the Netherlands in the late 80s/early 90s. He was very helpful and forthcoming and, what's more, he had story after story that either made me laugh or just shake my head in disbelief. After a few exchanges, it became evident that he had more than enough tales, anecdotes and opinions to write his own story.

As seems to be the case with many artistically talented people, their flair doesn't just manifest itself in a single outpouring. Theo's way of playing football – the creativity and vision he possesses – can also be seen in his art and he is an accomplished painter. Then again, he *is* Dutch. Think of the Netherlands and what immediately jumps to mind? Rembrandt and Cruyff, Van Gogh and Van Basten. There have been exhibitions of Theo's artwork in the Rijksmuseum Twenthe in Enschede and he has given talks there about the impressionists. If only he made cheese as well, that would be a whole national stereotype rolled up into one person!

Standing Free, though, is the story of Theo ten Caat the footballer. While he never quite hit the ultimate heights in footballing terms as in representing his country at World Cups and European Championships, he did ply his trade in the top leagues in the Netherlands and Scotland, played in European club competition and crossed paths – and sometimes swords – with some big names, including Erik ten Hag, Phillip Cocu, Paulo Futre and Diego Maradona.

His story is a fascinating one from the time he was a little boy growing up in the Netherlands' rural north-east to his current coaching work via an intriguing, captivating and sometimes controversial career in professional football. He talks about how he had to face some struggles as a young boy – not at trying to make it in football but with some ridiculously cruel and senseless treatment from people who really should have known better – along with his route through the professional game. One thing that stood out all the way through our meetings was, despite the fact that throughout his career he worked with some of his boyhood heroes and at some of the local and favourite clubs of his youth, his heart really is in Aberdeen. This shone through in our conversations and hopefully is manifested on to the pages of this book.

Theo ten Caat really is still Standing Free.

Growing Up and Getting
My Foot on the Ladder

*'I would hate to be third or fourth choice,' I
told him, 'so feel free to go and pick yourself
another captain.'*

I WAS born in the countryside in the region of Hollandscheveld
in the north-east of the country, not too far from the border with
Germany, where there were lots of farmers. My mother and
father were both children of the war. Like so many others, my
granddad had a problem coping with the war and never spoke
about it. Now that sort of thing is recognised and they call it
PTSD – post-traumatic stress disorder. It affected him pretty
badly. It's very sad.

My grandparents and my parents lived together in a small
house because there wasn't enough housing for everybody to
have their own place, as there was a big rebuild going on due
to what happened in the war. This meant that for my first few
years we were all sharing a house together.

We didn't have much materially when I was a boy and we
were never really able to go away on holiday. We did some day
trips, and they were nice, but we were never able to go on what

you would call a proper holiday. When my mum and dad were building a house they only managed to build the ground floor because the money ran out and the bank didn't want to finance them anymore. In the recession of the 1980s my dad became unemployed. I was 16 at the time and my brother and I always brought football boots that were two sizes too big so they would last us. My dad would put some cotton in the boots and stuff it down the end where our toes were so we could play in the same boots for a year or two extra.

My dad was only 40 when he became unemployed and had some problems with his back. He tried to get other work, of course, but because of these back problems he was unable to. When his benefit money ran out my mum had to go out to work. She was a trooper. She did everything. She worked in a cafeteria, she worked as a waitress, she worked helping out farmers in the fields, she was very hard-working. She also took care of my grandparents, cleaning their house, doing shopping for them, all those sorts of things.

When he was younger, my dad was a really talented footballer – he could have been a professional – and one or two clubs wanted to sign him. His parents, my grandparents, were a little bit difficult about it, though. They were Christians and, with the matches being played on Sundays, they didn't like him playing then. They held Sundays as a sabbath and, when he did go out, he used to have to leave his football boots with his neighbours rather than bring them back into the house so my grandparents didn't know he had been playing.

He was good enough that in the early 1960s he could have become a professional with PEC Zwolle. He joined up with them but after three months he went back home. He was actually offered a contract but decided against it. He was there by himself and didn't really have much support, so he went back home. For me, this turned out to be a good decision, because not long after he left Zwolle he met my mother, so had he decided to carry on and sign his contract I wouldn't have been here!

I was born in December 1964 and things were a bit different by then. I had a lot more chances to play football and, as soon as I could walk I was playing with a ball. There weren't very many houses around; our area had lots of fields and farmland, so there were plenty of places to go and kick a ball. When my brother Freddy was born in 1966 we moved into a town but only stayed there for a couple of years before moving back into the countryside and living between the farmers again.

I have another younger brother called Rene, who is a few years younger. He was born in 1970. Because of the age difference between us, whereas Freddy and I had helped each other to develop, Rene was too young to join in with us seriously. He was also talented, though, and played some reserve games for Emmen.

When I was a boy growing up I didn't have that many friends. This was partly due to my mum being worried about virtually everything and partly due to my being busy with playing football. The thing is, in every spare moment Freddy and I were out kicking the ball to one another. We played before school, we played after school, when we came home to have our lunch, whenever we had an opportunity. Living out in the countryside we were free to play football whenever we wanted to.

Reading this you might think I was a bit hard done by and lonely but that wasn't the case. Being able to play in this way was good for our development. If you're playing on your own, or with just a few of you, it's all about your character and quality and you develop your personality. This is a natural way of development between boys. You quickly find out things like who is the leader of your little group, who can play in the different positions, what kind of games we would play rather than just have a traditional match between us, those kind of things.

Our village was split in two. There were the Christian people and non-Christian people, but most of them were Christians. Because of this there was both a Saturday team and a Sunday team, and the Sunday team really hated the Saturday team. That hatred was even evident at school. There was a Christian school and a public school. Everyone was able to go to the public school but to attend the Christian school you had to belong to that part of the community and had to be a churchgoer.

This was the reason we had two teams. It was a ridiculous situation. In a place with fewer than 5,000 people living in it they couldn't get together to make one decent football team. Every so often the idea of merging would be suggested and voted upon but they would rather have the segregation. The members of each team hated each other, too. I remember my brother once saying, 'I hope the two teams do come together because it would only take one training session for this one particular guy to end up in hospital for a couple of years!' Those were the times I grew up in.

When I was graduating to under-12s, after a few training sessions the two coaches decided that they would make me the captain of the team. I was obviously pleased about this but I later found out from some of the other boys that they had already asked others to be captain before they offered it to me. I went home and told my dad what had happened and he asked what I wanted to do about it. Was I happy being third or fourth choice? I said to him that I was the best football player in the team. I was captain the season before with the under-10s but now I had been relegated down the list. I asked him if it was to do with the friendships and business ties between the coaches and the families of the other boys and he told me that, yes, that was the case. That same evening I went back to the training ground and threw the captain's armband back to the coach.

'I would hate to be third or fourth choice,' I told him, 'so feel free to go and pick yourself another captain.'

I was only 11 years old at that time but I couldn't stand it. I'm a bit of a perfectionist and want to be the best, and by that time I already had that attitude in me. There weren't a massive amount of people living in our area and I knew I was the best player. As I've already said, we were out in the country and there were only little towns nearby, with just a small amount of industry. There were primary and secondary schools but if you wanted to take your education any further you had to move away. That was the size of the area we were living in. It was really quite remote. I didn't really like going to school much, even though I was pretty good academically. After I finished my primary schooling I went to Hoogeveen to take my exams and had an opportunity to go to university. It was when I moved to the secondary school that my problems began.

In his younger days my dad was a fighter, a real fighter. If something he didn't like happened to him, then he would sort it out with his fists. There's a story that when he was a teenager, 17 or 18 years of age, he hit someone on their ear with an iron bar and the other guy's ear almost came away from his head. It was apparently half off, just flapping around. My mother didn't like that my father was a bit that way inclined and she always taught me that I shouldn't fight, and that made a big impact on me. Naturally your parents want what's best for you, so because of my mum I wasn't allowed to fight. Add to this the fact that when I was young my mum and dad couldn't speak proper Dutch. That may sound strange coming from a Dutchman, but they always used the local regional dialect of where they lived and where I was born. At my local primary school that wasn't a problem because it was the same for everybody, they were all using the local dialect. When I went to Hoogeveen, however, they were, of course, all talking Dutch.

Because of this problem with the language the other boys at school were always laughing at me because of the way I spoke. I was a small kid as well, really tiny, so for these reasons I tended to keep myself away from the groups and gangs of boys that would hang around together as they do at school. It was also for these reasons that I was bullied quite a lot, and with my mum bringing me up telling me not to fight, even if I was bullied, it was best for me to keep away from most of the other kids. My escape was football. This was my only way of winning the respect of all the other kids. They respected me as a football player because I was the best one there. When they were picking teams I was always picked first. Even among all the local teams – we didn't have any academies attached to clubs at that time, so everybody played together regardless of their talent – I was always the best. That was how I gained my respect among the other boys. On the football pitch it didn't matter that I wasn't talking Dutch. Those were the times when they saw the real Theo ten Caat.

Taking all of my circumstances into consideration – my height, the way I spoke, not being allowed to fight back – I had to have some form of self-defence so I created a big mouth for myself. I thought that, aside from my footballing ability, this could be the only weapon I had. Conversely, though, this is probably also another reason why I didn't have many friends, and they gave me nicknames, not very nice ones. In fact, it was only a couple of years ago that I almost did get into a fight because of it. I happened to bump into an old schoolmate of mine and he called me by one of my old nicknames. I said to him, 'You had better go now before I smash your teeth out of your mouth.'

Everything that happens in your youth shapes you as you grow up. It makes you who you are and what you become as a person. For example, my dad was obviously very proud of me when I started playing football and showed promise, but he would never congratulate me. He would never say that I played really well, even when I had. He would always say that I could do better and he gave me challenges – how many times could I keep the ball up in the air without it touching the ground, those sort of things. I have a bit of a feeling that because of the challenges that he had with my grandparents when he was a youngster and started playing football, he was focusing his own career on me and Freddy. In a lot of ways I can understand this.

There was another thing that really affected me in my youth that I still think about to this day. I had a cousin on my dad's side called Pedro who I was very close to. We lived in the same street and we used to hang out a lot together. He was just a few years older than me and had a big influence on the young me. We would play a lot together and he taught me how to ride a bicycle. I would go back to his house to his room and listen to his records, particularly Bay City Rollers and The Sweet. We were really good friends. He was like an older brother to me. One Sunday when I was 12 and playing for Hodo, my first youth team, Pedro and I stayed around after my game to watch the first team play and went into the cafeteria afterwards for a drink and a plate of chips. We were sitting around playing cards with a couple of other cousins and some friends. When it was time for me to leave Pedro said that he would stay for another half an hour or so and then go home for a bit before going round to my other cousins' to watch the football on the television, so I said that I would see him tomorrow. When he got home, he fell asleep on the couch and my aunt woke him up in time for him to go out to watch the football. On the way there on his bike he got hit by a car and was killed. He was just a teenager. That's how fragile and uncertain life can be. If my aunt had woken him up just a couple of minutes earlier or later that might not have happened.

When I woke up the following day, a Monday morning, my mum told me what had happened. I cried but still had to go to school. My dad was with my uncle, my mum was at home and I had to go to school because you have to do what society says. That's the reason I was sent in that day. It wouldn't have made any difference to my schooling whatsoever and they would have understood if I had stayed home but no, society says you have to go to school so I went to school. Then of course I had homework to do and then back to school the next day, so I didn't really have time to grieve. My mum and dad didn't allow me and my brothers to go to the funeral, that's how protective they were.

If you protect your son or daughter too much and take them out of every situation where they may have to put up some kind of fight or effort, then they don't learn anything. That's why I'm like I am with my son. He has of course been in situations where he's been facing problems and I've let him try to sort them out himself. Yes, of course I'll help him and give him advice, but I'm not going to take him out of every situation he ever gets in.

21

My mum and dad are the nicest people on Earth but they both avoid conflict.

I realise that my youthful experiences may be one of the reasons that I always seem to have issues with authority. I make my own choices and don't let other people make decisions for me about what I have to do. If there's something I don't agree with then I'm not doing it.

I also can't stand petty authority, and I guess it goes right back to the teachers who gave me a hard time. Along with those and the ones who laughed at my regional dialect, this is why I wanted to keep a low profile. I've also had a couple of coaches who were very authoritarian and would insist their ways were correct and we had to listen to them no matter what. I would much rather discuss issues, not on authority, but based on facts and opinions, and I always like to understand why the other person is thinking the way they are.

A lot of the time when I was at school I was afraid that they were asking me something and I didn't even realise they were because of my inability to speak proper Dutch. I can laugh at it looking back now but it's different when it's happening at the time to a boy of 13 or 14 years of age and all the other children are laughing at you. There was nothing wrong with my brain, it was just that I learned my local dialect rather than actual Dutch.

It's still the same today, in fact. Not with me but with my dad. Whenever he goes to Amsterdam and is ordering a cup of coffee the waiters often think he's an Englishman talking Dutch because of the accent he has. A lot of the pronunciation really is that different. It's like if you hear a German speaking English, you know immediately where they're from. That's what they think with my dad's accent. It's sad but it's true that many people, even in this day and age, still look at the region of Hollandscheveld and thereabouts as being not exactly a backward place, but not as good as them. It's looked at as a small town area where everyone is a farmer and doesn't know anything about modern-day living. It's up in the north-east, far away from The Hague and Amsterdam, and a lot of those people are arrogant towards us and still think they're higher class. It's not that they actually come right out and say it but you can just feel it in the way that they have opinions about you. In other places they do have a class system but we don't have that in Holland. However, the way that some people react to us being from up north where there's no industry and there are no universities would suggest they're all intellectual and we're all village idiots.

It was even worse when I was young. The world was a smaller place then. These days you've got the internet and long-haul travel and all the social media and everything else, but we didn't have any of that. We had a television with two or three networks, whereas now there are thousands. If I do a radio interview now I still hate listening to myself speaking in Dutch. If I'm in Scotland, though, I do it easily. Sometimes when I go to Amsterdam – and this is true – I just pretend that I'm Scottish. I don't want to talk Dutch to them. They think they rule the world but if you ask them what a potato looks like they don't know! They don't know that it's grown in the ground, they think it's grown in the local supermarket.

When we were growing up, my brother Freddy and I were always playing football and, because I was older, I was a bit more assured and so would attack him, and he always had to defend. We were always playing one against one. He had to defend all the time and I was attacking all the time. It was because of those little games between us that he became a defender and I became a more attacking player. While I was running at him trying to get past him, Freddy was trying to get the ball from me by tackling, by pushing or by adjusting his angles slightly to give him an advantage. It was natural for us. We actually played together professionally for a while at FC Twente. Unfortunately for Freddy, he picked up a big injury and it finished his career. He could have gone on to have a decent career in the game. You cannot say which one of us because we were totally different types of players. It's impossible to compare positions. Ironically, he would probably have done better at Aberdeen than I did because of his style of play.

My dad was a supporter of FC Twente because he had family living near there and as youths we always went to watch their games. We used to love going to the old stadium, buying our tickets out of a wooden hut. At that time they were a really good club. In 1975 they reached the UEFA Cup Final but were beaten by a really good Borussia Mönchengladbach team. They had players such as Allan Simonsen, Uli Stielike and

Berti Vogts, who was their captain. They were just too strong for Twente.

My hero was Epi Drost. He was a defender but would always do the craziest things in his own penalty box. He never just kicked the ball away. He would try to pass it clear or even just dribble out. Any tackles that came his way he would just take on, even in tight situations. He never seemed to want to take the easiest option. He played a few times for Holland in the early 1970s and actually became my first coach in professional football. He was assistant coach at Twente working with Fritz Korbach. I played under Epi for three months when I arrived there and we used to play chess together as well. Unfortunately, he suffered a cardiac arrest during a match in 1995 with some of his former international colleagues and died. He was voted as Twente's Player of the Century and he has a statue at the stadium.

Another two heroes of mine at Twente were Arnold Mühren and Frans Thijssen. The team really did have some midfield at that time with Mühren, Thijssen and Kick van der Vall. Arnold and Frans moved to England to play with Ipswich Town at the time when Bobby Robson was their manager. I remember the 1980/81 season when they were fighting for the title with Aston Villa. I had my own room then and every time Ipswich were playing I would tune in my transistor radio and receive the BBC football service. I would try to listen to the whole game just because Mühren and Thijssen were playing there. They had a really good team; it was a shame they didn't win the league championship but they did win the UEFA Cup. Ironically, they beat a Dutch team, AZ Alkmaar, in the final over two legs and Thijssen scored in each of the games.

Mühren was such a cultured player, he had silky skills, such a lovely touch. He went on to join Manchester United and scored in the 1983 FA Cup Final. Another of his greatest moments came in the European Championship of 1988, which Holland won. Everybody remembers that brilliant volleyed goal by Marco van Basten past Russian goalkeeper Rinat Dasayev in the final but it was Mühren who provided the cross for him.

As for Thijssen, I actually worked with him for a while when I was coaching at Twente. I was working with the under-19s and he was assistant manager of the under-21s. He was a really nice guy, modest, maybe a bit too modest in my opinion. I don't think he was really hard enough to be a coach. That being said, it's as a player that he'll always be remembered. He was a brilliant player, he really was. It's funny, we played for three of the same clubs – Twente, Groningen and Vitesse – and I only just missed having him as a team-mate every time!

I was 16 when I made my first appearance as a football player in the highest amateur league in Holland, with a team called VV Hoogeveen. When I moved there a couple of years previously I was *persona non grata* at my previous club. I was playing for Hodo, who were a local amateur team, and my move to Hoogeveen really didn't go down well with some of the people there. When I say 'didn't go down well' that was a bit of an understatement. I had people saying to me, 'Theo – I hope you break your leg.'

I was only 14!

These were grown-up people, adults, members of Hodo. It was absolutely disgraceful. If you think about it, what kind of crazy guys would do something like that? It's unbelievable. I won't name names, but members of Hodo actually said that they hoped I would break my leg after I moved to Hoogeveen. Can you imagine grown men saying that to a kid!? I still can't fathom it. I can only put it down to jealousy, their not wanting me to be successful. If they or their kids weren't going to make it then they would rather nobody did. It's a crazy way of acting.

A lot of things have changed there now but I can see that certain people have a problem with me and I have no idea why. Maybe it was because of their parents telling them stories from back in the day when I was playing there, I don't know. I mean, at my age I'm not going to be best friends with people in their 20s but even with the older generation I still feel a bit distant. I can only assume that it was because I had a successful career in football and they didn't make it. I find it quite strange and also quite sad. They never ask me back to help out with any training sessions or anything like that.

Most of my life – when I haven't been playing abroad – I've been living locally. Other teams from around the area have asked me to do certain things for them, but not Hodo. I've never been asked to do a clinic there or to do anything for the youth teams or even been asked for advice. My brother even played there for ten years because he had problems with his knee, but they just don't want to know me. I was a professional footballer for 18 years, but I might as well have never even existed. Sometimes there are people who are so arrogant – and this is everywhere, I'm not just singling out Hodo here – that they're afraid of power or what they see as power. If they see anybody who has more knowledge than they have they feel threatened.

Because of all those things – the bad wishes and then their ignoring me and, actually, maybe also because of my dad not having the greatest of reputations because of his fighting – I've just avoided them. Isn't that sad, avoiding my amateur team for such a long, long period? It's still a mental thing with me. Even if I think about it now it makes me angry. How the heck does a 30- or 40-year-old guy at the same club as I am tell me that he hopes I break my leg when I move on and play for another team? That's just hatred. When I left them I was still living for five years in the community and saw those kind of people around in the street, so I just tried to avoid them. When I moved back I didn't go to the village, because I didn't feel respected there. I stayed out of the way at my dad's place and hung around with my old friends, who are farmer friends. As a result, I never socialised among the people that had been so nasty to me before.

Even now I hardly have a social life here. Anyway, I'm busy coaching and doing my own football schools and boot camps. Every year there's a carnival here. It stays in town for a week, there's a lot of music and attractions and all the kids come and join in, all that sort of thing. One year there was a discussion about it at my boot camp.

'Theo, why don't you come along on the Saturday?' they asked.

I said, 'Well, I'm not really one for that sort of thing. I don't really drink alcohol and after an hour everybody is drunk!'

The discussion continued, so eventually I said, 'Okay, for you guys I'll go. For the boot camp team, I'll go. I'm in. On Saturday, let's do it.'

When Saturday came around I got there quite early and there were a few people there and they were asking why I've come because they don't usually see me there. I explained that the boot camp were all coming along. As the evening went on it turned out that all the boot campers came as individuals, not with each other. I thought it was going to be like a sort of team-bonding thing, which is why I agreed to go. Then after a while the first boot camper arrived and we said hello and exchanged the usual pleasantries, and then they said, 'Nice to see you, Theo, I'm off to find my friends now.'

And so it went on with five, six, seven others. They would come in, say hello and then go and find their friends! At some point I said to one of them, 'I'm here because of you guys, you talk to me for 30 seconds and then you go and find your friends. You're not even asking me to join you. What's going on? I came here for you because you wanted me to be here.'

I mean, I could handle it, I wasn't getting upset or anything, I just thought it was a bit odd. I thought we were here to all be together. As I've said, it isn't my idea of a fun evening out, going to a tent and watching people get drunk. Then I met somebody else that I knew and we had a chat, and then they said that they wanted to go in for a dance and that they hoped to see me again later on in the evening.

What was happening here? I was invited to come out with my boot campers, they all go their own way, I'm not being asked to join with their group of friends and there's absolutely no team bonding going on whatsoever! Walking back to my car I had to sit down because I just started laughing. I couldn't hold it in anymore, I was just laughing and laughing. We still talk about it to this day. We still make jokes about it.

Anyway, back to Hoogeveen. The level of football was much higher there, which made me choose to play for them. I was the youngest player and played for three years before going to FC Twente. We did well. We played on a Sunday and won the area championship and then beat the winners of the Saturday championship in the play-off to see who were the best team in the county. We beat them pretty easily, 4-0 or 5-0, and I scored three goals.

As had been the case at Hodo, there was also a bit of jealousy among the parents of the boys there. It was okay at first, but when I moved up to the under-17s that's when it began. There are two years of boys playing in that team: those who are 15 and those who are 16. Before I moved up there had been a certain balance in the team. As is the way in any team, if somebody else comes in, as I did, the balance changes a little and the best player isn't the best player anymore and that affects the culture of the team. The balance in the play and in the team changed and some of the parents couldn't handle it. I was small and quick but not particularly strong when it came to the more physical aspects of the game and, because I was little, the coach there used to tell the other players to 'just kick him'. I liked to dribble with the ball round all the bigger boys. They were growing their muscles, becoming men, but I was still very small. The coach told the others to kick me and so they did. Often, I would have blood inside my boots after the training session.

The physio of that team was a real pain. He had the same attitude as the coach. He would tell me I had to get rid of the ball sooner to avoid the challenges. Either that or fight them back.

After a while of this happening I said to my dad that I didn't want to play anymore and that I wanted to quit football. I stopped going for about three or four weeks. Then I started going again but quickly got injured. The physiotherapist of the first team heard about what had happened and took me under his wing. He knew about me being one of the most talented boys in the amateur team and wanted to know why I had stopped playing football when I did. I told him it had stopped being fun for me because I was lying on the ground more than I was playing football. The other boys were kicking me all over the place and the coach was telling them 'well done'!

When you're small you develop a certain way of playing football. When you're big you develop a certain way of playing football. When you're fast, you develop a certain way of playing football. So, because I was small and pretty quick, the way I liked to play back then was how I always liked to play when I became a professional. I was also very determined, probably because of the way I was brought up and having to put up with the things I had to go through when I was at school. I was a bit of a perfectionist as well. I always had to win the games I was playing in. Every game.

It was the physio who actually got me into the first team, and I'm very grateful to him for that. The system has changed now but at that time it was the highest level of amateur football throughout the country. It was the first time I was paid for playing football, 100 guilders a month. Another reason they tried me in the first team was, to be completely honest, because they weren't exactly very good at that time. So, what do you do? You bring in youngsters. I was 16 and in the first team and at the end of that season we were relegated, but it was my first connection with senior football.

Joop Oldejans came in as manager for the following season. Oldejans had been a professional player and coach and knew what he was doing. We didn't go back up as champions, we came second, but then FC Twente came in for me and asked me along for a trial. Epi Drost, my hero from when I used to go and watch them, was looking after the reserve team at that time, so that was a bit of a thrill for me. I played in a friendly match for the reserves, which I thought went okay, but they told me that I hadn't been good enough, so I went back to Hoogeveen for the next season. That season we won the league easily and Twente came in for me again. This time they also asked my brother Freddy to come along as well, so we did a trial together.

After that game the manager came to see me at my house, along with the head coach and the head of scouting, and told me that they wanted me and my brother to sign on for Twente. We agreed, of course, and tried to keep cool in front of them but, naturally, we were really excited. My mother, however, disliked the idea that we would go.

It was after I had decided I was going to sign for Twente that a scout from Ajax came to me and told me not to sign for Twente and to give it a go in Amsterdam instead. They had a really good squad at the time, a lot of young players who would go on to be greats. Stanley Menzo was the goalkeeper, they had players like Ronald Koeman, Frank Rijkaard, Jesper Olsen, Gerald Vanenburg, Marco van Basten and so on. A very attractive draw indeed but I told the scout that if Ajax wanted me they were too late, I had decided to join Twente.

FC Twente

'I am happy to announce that we have made a deal
with Theo ten Caat for another two years,' he told
everybody as part of his speech. 'What's happening here?'
I thought to myself. I didn't even know about this.

WHILE FREDDY and I were excited about going to Twente, our mother disliked the idea. The reason for her reticence was that we went into a guesthouse, staying with the family that lived there. To be honest, that was one of the biggest mistakes we made. I was 19, my brother was 17, and we really should have rented a place. Under the guidance of the manager, though, we stayed with this family. The club had a few places where they could house the young kids so they knew where they were and what they were doing.

That woman hated me. She liked my brother but she hated me because of my character. I was cheeky. I didn't hate her but she hated me. She said to me that I had to wash the dishes and I asked her why. I told her that she was making money from me so why should I do the dishes? I wasn't going to do the washing up so that she and her children could be free to go into the city to do some shopping. At the time I thought that was fair enough.

That was the kind of relationship that I had with her. Even her husband was afraid of her. He wasn't allowed to smoke but I knew that he was smoking secretly at the end of the garden. I know this because one day I caught him at it.

'Don't tell my wife,' he said, 'otherwise I'm in trouble.'

'Don't worry,' I said to him, 'I'm not going to tell your wife anything.'

We started with Twente on 14 July 1984. I'll never forget that date. I rode my bike to the stadium and walked into the players' lounge. They were all in there and I didn't really know what to do. I looked round and just sat down on the first empty chair I could see. A German called Fritz Korbach was the coach. I was already there when he arrived and he asked me if I had introduced myself properly to the other players. I was a shy boy at the time and told him that I hadn't, so he said that it was important that I did that. He made me go round the room and shake everybody's hand, telling them who I was. So, I went nervously round the room introducing myself, shaking all the hands.

We started training and, of course, I had to learn everything from scratch. This was a completely different level to what I had been used to. I even had to learn to carry my bag properly! They tested me in every possible manner. They put salt in my soup when I wasn't looking. When I was lying on the physio's table on my front, they put tape on my backside. You can imagine the discomfort when I pulled it off! All those kind of things I had to go through. Every training session I was getting kicked. I knew that this treatment was different from when I was getting kicked at Hoogeveen, however. I knew that his was because they were testing me, trying me out to see if I had what it took.

We had a training camp at Kaufbeuren in Germany, not far from Munich and near to the borders with Switzerland and Liechtenstein. It was a beautiful place. It was the first time I had ever seen mountains. We were staying in a hotel and playing games there and also in Austria. All this was completely new for me. It really opened my eyes to professional football and it was really hard work. I'll never forget that the hotel had a big staircase with a big rope on one side, like a fisherman's rope, like the rope they might use on the decking of a ship. We stayed there for two weeks and after the end of the first week I had to use the rope to pull myself up in order to get to the first floor, that's how hard it was. My body wasn't ready to train that hard. We would do 100m runs, then 200m then 400m. We had breakfast at 7.00, training at 10.00, lunch at 12.00, an afternoon nap, another training session at 3.00 and then sometimes a game in the evening. I had gone from training a couple of times a week to training two or three times in the same day. It was intense.

Jan Sørensen was our star player but he missed the training camp because he was on trial at Liverpool at the time. As it turned out he didn't get his transfer to Anfield as they signed Jan Mølby, another Danish international, from Ajax instead. Mølby went on to be a multiple league champion and became one of the best central-midfield players in Europe.

There was one occasion that I remember when I had booked a massage with our physio. Whether he actually had any qualifications to give massages, however, I don't know. What he used to do was ask two other players to come in and they would hold you down and then he would whack his elbow into your groin. Lovely! That's the kind of guy he was. So anyway, I had an appointment with him one afternoon to get a massage and I was lying on his table when Jan Sørensen walked in without an appointment and told me that I had to go.

'But Jan,' I protested, 'I have a massage booked in.'

Before Jan could answer, the so-called masseur walked in and he also told me that I had to leave and it wasn't my time yet. This left me a little confused.

'We had an appointment at 3.00,' I reminded him, 'and it's 3.00 now.'

'Yes, well, Jan is here now,' he countered, 'and the better players go first.'

That's how things went at that time. I had to get off the table and wait for Jan to finish before I could have my massage. That's just how it was, he was allowed to pull rank.

Aside from pulling rank and securing your place in the food chain, there were also lots of pranks and practical jokes that were being played, but that's how it is when a group of young men get together. Sometimes it can be hilarious, sometimes it can be silly and sometimes you can do things without really thinking it through or considering what the consequences might be. As an example of this, there was one time when André

Paus and Martin Koopman, two of our defenders, were in the little health centre area that we used to have. It was where the massage room was and there was also a sauna and the showers. Eric Groeleken, our centre-forward, came in to use the sauna. So, what Paus and Koopman did when they left, thinking it was funny, was to lock the door of the sauna. They didn't have the key so what they did was put a chair up against the door with the back of the chair wedged underneath the door handle so it couldn't be opened from the inside. Groeleken could see them walking away through the little glass window in the sauna door, realised that he was stuck inside and panicked. The only thing that he thought of doing was smashing the window, so he just punched it. He was furious. In doing so, he cut himself so badly that he had to go to the hospital. At first, Paus and Koopman had a laugh, but when they realised how serious it was it suddenly wasn't that funny anymore. Fortunately, there was no serious harm done.

My first season as a professional footballer was 1984/85. We had some good players in that Twente squad – Sørensen, Martien Vreijsen, Theo Snelders was in goal, Billy Ashcroft from England was centre-forward – we had some good players. That first year was pretty good. I scored six goals and we finished eighth in the table, which was a decent showing because the team had been promoted the season before.

For the first few months I was playing in the reserves under Epi Drost. We would play on the Saturday and the first team would play on the Sunday. We were playing against the reserves of Ajax, PSV, Feyenoord, all those teams, and we were top of the league. Then I got called to play in the first team.

My first actual professional game came on 31 October 1984. We were playing an away match at FC Den Bosch. With 15 minutes to go we were 3-0 behind and really had no chance of pulling the game back. I came on as a substitute, replacing André van Benthem, and that was my introduction into professional football. It's a shame the result wasn't better but Den Bosch had a good team that year, finishing only a few points out of the European qualification places. To be honest, looking back now, I don't really care about the result, what I care about is that it was my professional debut. Even if I never played another match again I could still say I was a professional footballer.

Having played in that game, I had a few weeks back in the reserves and sitting on the substitutes' bench before my first season really kicked off after the winter break. The next game I played in was at home against AZ Alkmaar and this time I was in the starting XI. The game finished in a 2-2 draw and I played the full 90 minutes. From then on I was in the team for the rest of the year. At the end of the season I finished fourth in the player of the year awards, which was pretty good for a young kid who had only just come into the team.

When the season ended I was out of contract but, as a member of the Professional Football League, I had an agent helping me out from the union. It was he who was doing the contract negotiations with FC Twente. The negotiations were a bit of a struggle because I wasn't making much at all, almost nothing, and even if you double nothing you still have nothing! With the contract negotiations ongoing, we had a bit of a party at the end of the season. All the players and their wives were there, the coaching staff, the board members, and there was music and food and it was a really nice evening. At some point during the evening, Ton van Dalen, the club's technical director, gave a speech.

'I am happy to announce that we have made a deal with Theo ten Caat for another two years,' he told everybody as part of his speech.

What's happening here? I thought to myself. I didn't even know about this.

What had happened was that during that day he had called my dad, made him an offer, whatever it was, and my dad had said, 'Yeah, that's okay, that's enough for Theo.' He had decided that I would accept the offer that the club had made without my even knowing what the offer was that the club had made! I mean, without being a particularly big deal, for a boy of 20 at that time it was a decent wage, but I still can't believe that my dad closed the deal without even letting me know what it was. Nowadays, a boy of 20 in that position would be receiving a contract that will be putting him on his way to being a millionaire, but then I hardly had a couple of thousand in my savings account.

So, when Van Dalen made this announcement at our party, you can imagine the shocked look on my face. All the boys were laughing, and even more so when he let everybody know that the agreement had been made with my dad. I didn't have the guts to say anything about it, to say that my dad wasn't actually my negotiating agent, because I was a shy boy.

The next season, 1985/86, there was a bit of a shuffle in the playing staff, a few players came in, a few players left. Jan Sørensen joined Feyenoord, Manuel Torres went to Valencia and Billy Ashcroft went back to England. One player we did sign was Gordon Hill. He had been a big player for Manchester United and also represented England. Gordon had been part of the team that won the FA Cup in 1977 when United beat Liverpool 2-1. He was playing with people like Steve Coppell, Martin Buchan and Lou Macari, so that shows you how good he had been. Unfortunately for him he picked up an injury that curtailed his career somewhat and he came to Twente with one knee, but even then you could see he was a great player. He could barely run but everything he did with the ball was brilliant. It was obvious why he had become a big star for Manchester United. He was one of those people that you just needed to see walk on to the pitch and you knew they were class. He made a big impact and I had a good relationship with him, even though he only stayed at Twente for a short time. He has since opened a soccer school in Florida, so he certainly chose his location well!

That summer we were playing in the Intertoto Cup competition. At that time there were cash prizes on offer and it wasn't until UEFA took over the running of the competition in 1995 that the winners received a place in that season's UEFA Cup. The competition was scrapped altogether in 2008. We were in a group of four with Standard Liège of Belgium and two German teams, Fortuna Düsseldorf and Rot-Weiss Erfurt. At that time Germany was still divided into East and West; the Berlin Wall didn't come down until 1989.

When we went to East Germany to play Erfurt, we might easily have had to return home a player light. On the way there we were told that when we crossed the border from West Germany we had to behave. It was strange crossing the border. We exited West Germany and then drove for about a kilometre and there was absolutely nothing there. No trees, no landscape, nothing. Just road.

When we got to the border we had to give our passports in to the manager so he could just give them to the border guards rather than all of us doing so individually. We had been told to behave because the East Germans were very strict and wouldn't take any nonsense from us. We were told in no uncertain terms that if we didn't behave we would have a problem. Having been told that, Ulrich Wilson, a defender who had joined us from Ajax, where he hadn't quite made the grade, decided that he would be the funny guy. He ducked down in his seat on the team bus and hid from the border guard. When the guard counted all the passports and then all the heads on the bus there was, of course, one head too few. He started to panic and shout, thinking that maybe one of our players had for some reason just run off, maybe trying to gain some kind of political asylum or whatever. He counted again and again but was still getting the wrong number of people to passports and getting himself into more and more of a state. Then, all of a sudden, Ulrich Wilson jumped out.

'Hello, here I am,' he said, smiling and laughing as he appeared from under his seat.

Needless to say, the border guards didn't think it was as funny as Wilson did. They made us park our bus and we had to wait a couple of hours while they thoroughly checked us all out, not just Ulrich, and we were allowed to carry on. He was lucky he wasn't arrested.

The next game was in Belgium against Standard Liège so we stayed in West Germany for a couple of days, setting up a little training camp in the Eifel, a low mountain range on the Germany/Belgium border about a couple of hours from Liège. One day we had a little training session in the morning, some lunch and then we went out for a walk. Not too long a walk, only about 45 minutes. Off we went into the forest in good spirits, but we somehow managed to get lost. Our 45-minute walk turned into a hike of more than four hours before we somehow found our way back to the hotel. Being lost and trying to find your way around for four hours is bad enough, but in a forest!? What sort of landmarks are you going to look out for? Trees? If you're lost in a forest, then you're lost. You've not really got an idea in which direction you're going, whether you're heading north or south. Eventually we managed to get back, more by luck than good orienteering.

During the camp we had one night off when we were allowed to have a drink, but it still had to be in the hotel. I didn't drink alcohol at that time and Marcel Fleer, our second goalkeeper behind Theo Snelders, who also wasn't a drinker, decided that he would try the Jägermeisters. He obviously liked them and got drunker and drunker and drunker and almost went into a drunken coma. The next morning at training, Fritz Korbach was having none of it. His attitude was 'if you're a man in the evening, you're a man in the morning', so he just carried on as normal, refusing to take Fleer's delicate condition into consideration. He had him at training as normal in goal, feeling awful, hungover and with a high temperature. This was going to be one of the hardest sessions of the camp but Korbach just got on with it. We had 200-metre sprints, muscle exercises, everything. How Fleer got through it I'll never know.

Not only that, but the evening before, when Fleer was on the Jägers, four of the other players decided that they would escape the confines and go to the little village down the hill. I think there was Martin Koopman, Michael Birkedal, Evert Bleuming and Martien Vreijsen. They were down in the village partying in a bar or a nightclub and then suddenly the door opened and look who came in – the coach, Fritz Korbach and his assistant. They tried to hide, of course, but they had been spotted. Whether the coach had been tipped off or whether it was pure coincidence I don't know.

'Hi boys, how's it going?' asked Korbach. 'All right, let's party.'

So they just joined them and the drinking went on into the night. When it was time to go back, Korbach reminded them that they weren't allowed to leave the hotel and thanked them for their hospitality in paying the bill. Of course, the players couldn't possibly argue so they paid not only their own tallies, but those of the two coaches as well. They must have thought that they had got away quite cheaply just having to pay for a few extra drinks after they had broken the rules.

Next morning at breakfast, Fritz Korbach stood up.

'Well, boys, we had an understanding but there were four players who went down to the village to party. Those players I'm giving a fine of 500 guilders.'

How it worked was that every day at the training camp the players were given 50 guilders to spend how they liked. This particular camp lasted for ten days so the 50 guilders fine meant that the four players ended up with nothing. That's how Fritz Korbach was.

We played Liège and were beaten 1-0 and then had to play Fortuna Düsseldorf. Even though the Intertoto was a proper tournament, it was still pretty much a friendly one, but they took it so seriously. They were flying into the tackles, putting themselves about a bit, as if we were playing in the European Cup. The main purpose for us was to get ready for the new season.

'Come on lads,' I said to one of their players, 'this is only a friendly tournament.'

'Wie spielen nicht für Käse,' was the response – 'We don't play for cheese.'

After the game, we went into Fortuna's dressing room. There were needles everywhere. I don't know what was in them, and I'm not insinuating that they were taking anything illegal, but even for friendly games they were taking it so seriously. Maybe injecting the players with cortisone. I mean, I have had cortisone injections myself as well but only when I was injured and needed something to relieve a bit of pain. It seems that they were just doing it before games. This wasn't an isolated incident, either. I've seen it many times. I've played against Dortmund, Köln, Düsseldorf, Schalke, etc., and every time we went into the dressing room it was the same. There were needles everywhere. It was unbelievable the way the players saw the games, even the friendly games. All the players were desperate to play because if they didn't they could lose their place in the team. That was their mentality. It wasn't until later that I saw the importance of not getting injured, otherwise there were other players who were waiting to take your spot. That was always the attitude of the Germans.

The Intertoto Cup was a bit of a strange thing back then as there were no actual competition winners. From 1969 until 1994, there were group stages and that was it. After we had all played each other, Rot-Weiss Erfurt had gained the most points and topped our little league but didn't then play knockout against the other group winners, the competition just stopped. Górnik Zabrze of Poland were declared the overall winners due to their having won their group with the best record of all the group winners. A very strange set-up.

After the Intertoto games and before the league season kicked off, we came over to Scotland to play Rangers in a friendly at Ibrox. It was my first trip over to the UK and it was a beautiful experience for me apart from that they beat us 2-1! Our tour lasted for a couple of weeks and, as well as Scotland, we visited France and Italy, where I came face to face with Diego Maradona in Naples.

Napoli had a great team at that time. Maradona, of course, was the main man, the star attraction, but they had good players all over the pitch, lots of internationals. Ciro Ferrara and Salvatore Bagni played for Italy and Daniel Bertoni was Maradona's mate from Argentina. A really good team.

The first day when we arrived there we were looking round the city, having a nice walk along the boulevard near to the sea, when this thing just run out past us. I thought it was a dog but it turned out to be a rat. I've never seen a rat that big. I honestly thought it was a little dog. The second day we went to the training ground, which was right near a mountain, and it was in such poor condition that you would think twice before letting your dog (or rat) run around on it. If you could play football and control the ball on that, you could play on a nice flat grassy pitch easily. And the fans, they were something else. They were already getting excited for the game, out in the streets in their cars and on their scooters, beeping their horns and making lots of noise shouting at us. It was as if we were playing against them in a cup final, not just a pre-season friendly. And this was the day before the match!

When the time for the game came round we were all really looking forward to it, not least because we would be sharing the pitch with Maradona. The thing is, during the game a lot of our guys were looking up to him, it was like they were star-struck. He just had this aura about him and we were giving him far too much space, which annoyed me.

We came together a few times on the pitch and I had to do everything I possibly could to try to stop him. At one point he tried to just run past me with the ball, which I knew he wouldn't be able to do because running was one of my strong points, I was always quite quick. So, because he couldn't get past me, he started to pull my shirt. The referee didn't whistle for this offence, so I turned around and just pushed him and he almost fell to the ground. We had a little bit of a pushing match over the ball, and when the referee arrived I tried to explain to him in English that it should be my free kick because he was pulling my shirt. Unfortunately, it seems that the referee didn't speak any English so I couldn't communicate with him properly, so I turned to Maradona and he turned to me and we squared up to one another. A couple of players from Twente and a couple of players from Napoli came over to intervene. I told my team-mates to get lost and keep out of it because I could handle myself and they had been scared to get near him all game so leave me to it now. So, it turned out that there was me in the middle of five or six Italian players. Did it really take that many to defend him? I'm not that scary! Not only was I surrounded by the Italians but the crowd was going mad as well and some of them even got on to the pitch and were heading towards us before the referee finally managed to calm things down.

As far as the match went, it finished 0-0. How we got a draw, I don't know as they must have had 90 per cent of the play.

So that was my encounter with Maradona and it was, don't forget, when he was entering his prime years. At the end of that season he inspired Argentina to the 1986 World Cup. He was absolutely brilliant during that tournament. Everyone remembers the goals he scored against England – both of them for different reasons – but he didn't just do it in that game. He destroyed Belgium in the semi-final, scoring another goal similar to when he walked through the English defence in the quarter-final, and he also played well in the final. Even though he didn't manage to score in that game, he was such a distraction for the German defence that because of it the other players had more room and they won 3-2.

That second year was a bit more difficult for me. To make the breakthrough into a team, as I had the season before, is easier than staying in the team because you have to keep at a certain level week in, week out. In a player's career, especially in the early part of their career, you don't see straight lines, you see ups and downs. They perform really well and then drop off for a bit before regaining their form again, and that's normal. I was still staying with the same family, I was doing my final exams at college and I also had a girlfriend at that time, who's now my wife, so it was a really busy time for me in all aspects of life. I was earning 10,000 guilders a year at the time and also had a car – that was big money for me. There were other players coming into the squad as well, so I had a bit of an in and out year. Funnily enough, most of the good games I played were against the top teams, the likes of Ajax and Feyenoord. In all honesty, it wasn't a very good season for us and we finished in the bottom half of the league.

For my final season at Twente, Fritz Korbach's contract came to an end and wasn't extended so Kees Rijvers came in as technical director and Theo Vonk was appointed the new head coach.

Rijvers was a very famous and experienced coach, having spent some time with PSV, where he won three league titles and the UEFA Cup, as well as a few years in charge of the Dutch national team when he introduced players like Ruud Gullit, Marco van Basten and Ronald Koeman to international football. He was also an international as a player. Vonk was a former player with AZ Alkmaar and he joined us after he had been managing Sparta Rotterdam.

I got married that year, so finally left the family who hated me – well, the mother in the family did – and we moved into our own place. My brother Freddy was also playing for Twente by then and actually he moved into our house with us, so there were three of us there.

I learned a lot from Kees Rijvers, he was a master. The team performed a lot better on the pitch than it had in the previous season and everyone was happy. In the winter break, during the early part of January, Rijvers came up to me and asked if we could talk, the two of us and Theo Vonk. So, the following day after a training session the team went out for a nice walk, and he came up to me again.

'Theo,' he said, 'we really appreciate your performances for the team and we would like to talk to you after lunch.'

So, we met up after lunch, and he said once again that they were happy with the way I was playing and that they could see that I was growing both as a football player and as a person. I was taking on more responsibility on the field and helping my brother, and I was married now, and he said that they would like me to settle down there and sign a new contract. He offered me another three years.

'You can make another 3,000 guilders more,' he said.

'Thank you,' I replied, 'but I hope you're talking about 3,000 more a month, not over a year.'

He looked at me and he said, 'It's over a year.'

'Excuse me,' I answered, 'I'm playing in my third season now and, by your own admission, am doing pretty well. I've played almost 60 games for the club, I think you're satisfied with me, and you're offering me 3,000 over a year?'

I was only making 20,000 guilders and now I had to pay for my own house. Fortunately, I had my brother there, who was also paying some rent, but what I was making was going straight out on the house and I wasn't able to save anything.

'If you were in my shoes,' I put to him, 'what would you do?'

He paused a bit before answering. 'I'm not in your shoes, Theo. It's your decision.'

There was hardly much of a decision to make.

'I'm not going to talk to you about this anymore unless you make me a better offer. If you cannot make me a better offer then I cannot play with FC Twente anymore.'

The problem here was that this was all before the Bosman ruling so, at that time, even when your contract came to an end you were still owned by the club and any other team that wanted to come in and buy you had to pay compensation, even though you were out of contract.

Not long afterwards there was a team meeting because, when the matches resumed after the winter break, the results weren't too good and it seems that there were one or two players who were thinking about leaving the club. Everybody was there at the meeting. Fred Rutten was the captain then. He was a terrible captain, not because he was a terrible player, but because he was friends with the coach. There's nothing wrong with everybody getting on, of course, in fact they need to, but for some players to be too close to the coach can cause divisions. And he wasn't the only one. Theo Snelders was my friend but he was also friends with both Fred Rutten and the coach. Martin Koopman – friend of the coach. André Paus – friend of the coach. Between them they were discussing everything. They were meeting up together at their houses outside of training and all the other players knew it. Because of this the atmosphere at the meeting was terrible. We knew that the coach was talking to the captain and these other players about the rest of us, so they were blaming us for the team's misfortunes.

We had also been knocked out of the cup by Excelsior, the ironic thing being that it was Jan Sørensen who had scored their winning goal after he had been loaned to them by Feyenoord. After that match Erik Groeleken, one of our midfield players with whom I also played at Groningen, had given an interview to a newspaper that the coach wasn't very happy with and he was disciplined for it.

'Whoever bounces the ball can expect that the ball is bouncing back,' Groeleken said to me after the coach had told him off.

'He knew that after what he had said in the newspaper his time was up at Twente.

So we had this meeting and everyone was sitting round listening to the coaches saying their bit and suddenly Theo Vonk said in my direction, 'And you Theo, you've destroyed the contract with your home because you don't want to play here anymore.'

'Excuse me,' I answered back, 'don't start blaming me, you have to look in the mirror. We had a meeting about that, didn't we? How much more did you offer me? You can tell it to all the boys here …'

'3,000,' he said.

The boys looked at me. '3,000 a month, Theo, why didn't you sign?'

I said, 'No, 3,000 a year!'

At that the boys started laughing and the trainers went mad, but we just ignored them and began to talk among ourselves.

'If that's all they're going to offer you lot as well,' I said, 'that would be an insult.'

By this time the meeting had completely fallen apart. The other players were saying that you only get the good money if you're friends with the coach and that everybody knew who his favourites were. Then somebody asked why I cancelled the contract with my house and I looked directly at the manager and said, 'One guess.'

Nobody dared to have that one guess, so I told them, still addressing Kees Rijvers. I was really fed up by now so I really let him have it.

'It's obviously down to the money I make and because I can't take any bonuses anymore. Last year, if you were a sub or sitting in the stand injured, you still earned your bonus, with minimum bonuses a year of 15,000 guilders. This year you changed it. There is no minimum bonus anymore, you have to actually be playing in the game to get it. If you're on the bench you get 75 per cent. If you're in the stand you get 50 per cent. You're punishing us twice. First because you don't give us all of the money that we deserve because we train as much and as hard as the ones that you pick for the team, and second because you don't play us. We're football players and make our money by playing football. We are our own business so, if we're not playing, the value of our business goes down. This means that I'm not able to live in my house anymore, it's too expensive for me. That's the reason I cancelled my contract. I don't want to leave FC Twente but I have to because, in effect, you're taking money away from me.'

I was only 22 at that time and I was standing up not just for myself but for all the other players as well. I stood up and said to the coaching staff that the way they were treating us stinks. By the time that meeting ended I knew that my days at FC Twente were finished.

Rene Roord came up to me afterwards and said that I was right to say what I did. It wasn't what I wanted to hear.

'You can shut up,' I told him, 'because you should have said that in front of everybody five minutes ago. Nobody has an opinion, nobody wants to express themselves, and that's why we're losing games. We're not a team.'

Rene is now the technical director of the FC Twente women's side and his daughter Jill plays for the national team. As a player he was really unlucky because he broke his leg when he was a young and never recovered from it.

When I got home I told my wife that that was it, I would be out of the club. They didn't offer me another contract because they were fed up with me, not as a player, but as a person because I was the only one brave enough to stand up to them about their misbehaviour towards us. And I was only a kid of 22 years of age. It crossed my mind that this could be it for me in professional football so I started thinking about what I could do outside of the game while perhaps playing as an amateur or semi-professional. I had a few interviews with some companies but, when it became known that I was leaving Twente, Veendam came and spoke to me. It was then that Henk Nienhuis, who had recently been appointed as their manager, did an absolutely brilliant thing. Veendam had a very talented player called Peter Huistra, who was on loan to them from Groningen. With Nienhuis knowing that I was leaving Twente, he somehow managed to set up a swap deal with me going to Veendam and Peter Huistra going the other way to Twente. The thing was, Huistra wasn't actually his player, he belonged to Groningen! It's unbelievable. How he got away with it I'll never know. Perhaps that should have told me that my time at Veendam was going to be, shall we say, *interesting* …

Veendam

I sat on the pitch and had cramp all the way up my legs, from my toes to my backside, on both legs. I couldn't walk, I was completely gone.

JOINING VEENDAM meant that I dropped down a league and became a semi-professional, whereas I had been a full professional in the highest league with Twente. This might have made some players dig their heels in and wait for other offers, but I didn't care. I knew I wouldn't play for Twente again and just wanted to get on with the rest of my life.

The club had organised a job for me with a big transport company where I worked in the office dealing with invoices and payments for the company's clients, which meant that my days became very long and intense. I was leaving home at seven in the morning to drive to Veendam to start working at my job and then, after eight hours there, training started at five in the evening. Sometimes it would begin a bit later because the coach, Henk Nienhuis, was also the chairman so he was always busy doing something.

On the football front we did pretty well that year. I was the captain of the team and we finished second to RKC Waalwijk, who had more money so could therefore afford better players. Veendam operated on a very low budget so actually we did really well to finish second.

I said that my time at Veendam would turn out to be, shall we say, *interesting*, and one particular incident during that season jumps to mind. Towards the end of the season we had an important game against Waalwijk coming up, the first-placed team against the second-placed team, with the team in third only just below us. The way the league worked was that the champions and runners-up would be promoted into the Eredivisie, so it was important for us to have a good game. Unfortunately, in the lead-up to the game I was ill. I had a throat infection with a fever and a high temperature and couldn't really get out of bed. The manager, however, was asking me how I was every day and I kept telling him the way I was feeling and the state I was in I really didn't see how I would be able to play. He kept insisting that I needed to be okay because it was a really important match, first against second, and they needed me out on the pitch. I told him that I would do my best but would have to see how I was on the Saturday. During the week I wasn't really able to do much, just lying around taking my antibiotics and that was about it. As the weekend approached I started to feel a bit better, although I still wasn't able to train on the Friday. With the match scheduled for Saturday evening, Henk Nienhuis called me on Saturday morning to see how I was.

'I'm not feeling good,' I told him. 'I don't think I can play.'

'Give it another couple of hours,' he said. 'Get something good to eat and see how you go.'

Two hours later we were on the phone again.

'Just come down to the club,' he said, 'but bring your boots just in case.'

So I had something to eat and went to the ground, still feeling pretty bad. We had a team talk about how to approach the game and what tactics to use and this and that, and I was expecting somebody else to be named the captain for the evening. It turned out, though, that I was in the squad!

'Hang on,' I interjected, 'we didn't discuss this. I can't play. I haven't trained all week. I've only just got out of bed after being ill and I'm still not feeling that well.'

'Well, you're on the list,' was his reply. 'Put your boots on, this is a really important game. If you only play ten minutes then you play ten minutes, but you're going to start anyway.'

Having heard this I went to the dressing room with the boys and had a talk with the assistant manager. I told him what I had previously told Nienhuis, that this was ridiculous and wouldn't be healthy for me. I said that I'd had a throat infection and was on antibiotics and now I have to play a really important game. He said that maybe I should see the club doctor.

In normal circumstances that would have been a perfectly sensible thing to do but we had a crazy medical staff at Veendam. As well as working for the club, the doctor had his own practice, so he spent most of his time there. He would come to the club on a Friday and have a look at the players at the training session then. Our physio – well, calling him a physio was overstating it a bit – was just lazy and he didn't seem to want to do anything. We had a really good team but the organisation of things certainly left a little to be desired. Well, I say a little, it left a lot to be desired!

The doctor sat next to me and we had a little chat and he told me to just take it easy, do my warm-up, take a shower and just sit on the bench doing nothing watching the game. So I went out and went through a bit of a warm-up, and after about ten minutes I felt myself going dizzy. It wasn't good. I was almost throwing up. I went back over to the doctor.

'I don't think it's going to work,' I told him. 'My head is shaking, I'm almost throwing up, there's no way I can play. If I have to sprint 20 or 30 yards I'm going to go down.'

'Okay,' he said, 'no problem, come with me.'

'Where are we going?'

'We're going back to the dressing room.'

I walked off the pitch, just following him like a dog back to the dressing room. The Veendam stadium was old and inside there was just one corridor with our dressing room on one side and the opponents' dressing room just across the way. It was so close that if you listened carefully you could hear what was going on, not only with the opposition, but almost in the whole building! When we got into our dressing room he closed the door behind us and I went to sit down on the wooden benches that went round the walls.

'No, Theo, you're not going to sit down here,' he told me.

'Really?' I was surprised. 'What am I doing then?'

'We're just going to the physio's room.'

'Why am I going there? I'm not going to play ...'

'You just come with me.'

I followed him into the physio's room and the first thing he said was to close the door. So I closed the door.

'That's not what I meant, Theo,' he said.

Hang on – I've followed him into the dressing room, closed the door behind us, gone through to the physio's room and closed the door behind us again and now he says that isn't what he meant. What's going on?

'Lock the door,' was the next instruction.

'Are you serious? Lock the door? What's going on?'

The physio's room was small and there were various medications and massage oils and everything around the walls, but he ignored everything that was already there. He opened his doctor's bag and was fiddling around inside it and then he told me to turn around.

'What do you mean?' I asked.

'Turn round,' he said, 'with your hands on the physio's bench and pull your shorts down.'

'Are you serious?'

I turned round and looked at him and he was holding one of the biggest needles I've ever seen.

'What are you going to do with that?' I asked him, dreading the answer.

'What do you think I'm going to do with it?' he replied.

'Hang on,' I told him horrified, 'there's no way you're going to—'

And then he just hammered it into my backside. I'd had injections before and wasn't afraid of needles but this one hurt! This needle was big.

'There you are,' the doctor said, 'now put your shorts on, take a drink of water, take these pills and wait for five minutes.'

What the pills were I don't know, I can't even remember how many he gave me – it could have been a couple, it could have been half a dozen. I did as he said, waited five minutes and then went out to the pitch, and by now the place was crowded. It wasn't a big stadium but it was a sell-out and there was a really great atmosphere. I made myself ready for the game but by now I was a bit bothered by what had just happened. I hadn't expected any of this but went out to join the boys anyway. I went over to join Henk Veldmate, who went on to be the chief scout at Ajax and director of football at Groningen, but he said the warm-up was almost done. We just had time to do the last couple of exercises and then we went back in again for our last little team talk before kick-off. The doctor was sitting in there and he gave me a wink and asked how I was feeling.

'I have to say, doc, that I do feel a bit better than I did ten minutes ago.'

'I told you, Theo,' he said, and he gave me another drink of water and some tablets for my headache. I don't know whether I had the headache due to my sickness, because of the other pills he had given me or just the stress of it all.

When we went out and kicked off, it was a really intense game but, to my surprise, I felt really good. I could run, I could tackle, I could dribble and make my crosses and I played a pretty good game. During the second half, with the score at 2-2, which we were happy with due to Waalwijk being a better team than us, after about 70 minutes, I just fell down. I just collapsed. One moment the sky was blue, the next there was darkness. I sat on the pitch and had cramp all the way up my legs, from my toes to my backside, on both legs. I couldn't walk, I was completely gone. The doctor came on to see to me.

'At least you lasted 70 minutes,' he said. 'You can say what you want about me but I'm a pretty good doctor!'

And that was that – game over. The doctor and the physio carried me off the pitch between them and took me straight to the dressing room. The match finished 2-2 and we were happy with a point.

The following day, the Sunday, I started to feel sick once more. My throat was sore again and I missed another week of training. The next game was away at Excelsior and the same thing happened leading up to that game. I trained on the Friday but this time Henk Nienhuis said he wouldn't take any chances with me, but then said I needed to bring my kit and boots to the game. Stupidly, I did exactly that. I took everything with me and – would you believe it – I was in the squad again. Fortunately, I wasn't as bad as the previous week and didn't need to see the doctor this time. This game also finished in a draw and I was taken off at half-time. The only good thing I did in the entire half was to set up the goal. For the other 44 minutes I did nothing. I couldn't run, I could barely control the ball, nothing.

I've never since had a discussion with the doctor about his treatment and neither have I spoken with the physio or Henk Nienhuis because I'm pretty sure that the doctor didn't tell anybody what happened. It didn't happen to any of the other players during my time there, or at least not that I know of. As I said, I don't know what the doctor gave me or injected into me but it was a pretty miraculous cure, at least temporarily until the day after the game when I felt bad again.

That season we played some really good games, especially at home in front of our own crowd. Personally, I was playing really well, scoring goals and making assists, but I still remember that the crowd at Veendam was crazy. I remember one game when after just a couple of minutes I played a pass that was wayward and ended up in the crowd. Some of the people starting shouting at me and enquiring not so politely if I would like to go back to Twente. I actually turned to the crowd and answered them.

'Guys,' I said, 'I've already scored six goals and provided many assists and now after three minutes you give me stick? Come on …!'

The crowd was so close to the pitch that we could hear what they were saying and I could hear them laughing at me. The away fans were always having a go at us. I could have started a grocery shop with all the apples and pears and things thrown at me when I was taking a corner.

I scored a hat-trick in the game against Emmen that eventually promoted us. That game was on a Saturday and on the Sunday both De Graafschap and Maastricht, who were close behind us in the table, were beaten so we gained promotion. It would have been nice to have secured the promotion out on the pitch and had a celebration out there with the fans but promotion is promotion.

After we had obtained our place in the Eredivisie, FC Groningen came in to sign me. That year they hadn't had a particularly good time and had finished in only eighth place. At that time, the teams who finished fifth, sixth, seventh and eighth played off to see who would qualify for European football. The deciding game turned out to be FC Twente against FC Groningen and I went to watch the match knowing that the following year I would be a Groningen player. Groningen won the game and, even though I had always been a Twente supporter, I was really happy because it meant that I would be playing in Europe after my move.

FC Groningen

There was steam coming out of my ears. I went
straight back to speak with the manager again.
'What is happening here?' I demanded, 'you're
running my career now.'

I HAD three really good seasons at FC Groningen, we had a
good team. Two of the three seasons we also played in Europe. We
had a coach called Hans Westerhof who came from an amateur
team called ACV – Asser Christelijke Voetbalvereningen – who
were based in Assen, which is just south of Groningen. He had
done very well there, winning a couple of championships in
the Hoofdeklasse, which is the second-highest-ranked amateur
league in the country. Even though he'd had success at ACV,
moving to Groningen was still a big step for him. It was his
first professional job but it proves how well he did because he
moved on to PSV Eindhoven and Ajax after. He also went over
to Mexico for a while.

We had a good team with some good players like John
de Wolf, who came over to the UK to play with Wolves in
England, René Eijkelkamp, who went on to PSV and played for
the Dutch national team, and Mr Groningen himself, Jan van

Dijk. He played pretty much his entire career at the club and also went on to manage them. They had qualified for Europe before I joined them, so that was a nice bonus for me to have a chance to play in the European games.

My first European game was a big one, a home tie against Atlético Madrid in the UEFA Cup, which has now been revamped and rebranded as the Europa League. Atlético had some really good players in their team. Paulo Futre, the Portuguese winger, was one of their star men along with Baltazar, who was a Brazilian international at the time. We won the first leg in Groningen 1-0, Eric Groeleken scoring the goal. It was a tremendous free-kick goal from 30 yards. How we managed to win that game I'll never know, the free kick was pretty much our only decent chance of the match. If we were to play that game a further ten times we would probably lose nine of them, such was Atlético's dominance. We were a bit naive and played so open that after we scored the whole game was played in our half of the pitch. They hit the post, the crossbar, shots were going just wide. Fortunately, they kept missing their chances and somehow we held on for the victory. It was an incredible game.

For the second leg we went over to Madrid to the Vicente Calderón Stadium, which was their home at the time before they moved to the Metropolitano, where they play now. We went over a couple of days before so we had some time in Madrid where we could do some sightseeing or some shopping, everyone doing their own thing. I went into one of the local shops with a couple of the lads and the guy in there told us we didn't have a chance against Atlético in the second leg. He confidently said it would be 4-0 or 5-0 or something. It was all friendly and we were joking around and I said to him, 'I promise you I'll score a goal.'

When the game kicked off, Futre got the ball and walked through everyone into our penalty box and there was a foul on him, so they were awarded a penalty. Baltazar scored and we were a goal down after one minute. Remembering what happened in the first leg and how good they had been, we all thought we were in for a long night. They continued to put pressure on us and we were a bit fortunate at times but slowly came into the game. After 20 minutes I kept my promise to the man in the shop. I scored the equaliser, probably the biggest goal of my career so far. Even though in the game Atlético were putting us under an awful lot of pressure, we were now in the driving seat, being 2-1 up on aggregate.

At half-time we found out that John de Wolf had sustained a broken toe during the first half and he was very sore, but there was no way he was coming off the pitch as he was one of our best players. So that made the second half a little bit harder for us, him not being 100 per cent, but he soldiered through, having had injections in his toe at half-time. He couldn't walk for a couple of weeks afterwards but he was fine about that because he had played against such a big team in such a big stadium. Atlético scored again in the second half to make it 2-1 thanks to Futre and then had other chances, but we battled and battled. We defended so well, just tackling and blocking, not really playing football but keeping them out. Every time we broke up an attack we just knocked the ball forward to our two strikers, Henny Meijer and René Eijkelkamp. At the end we lost the game 2-1 but, even though we were beaten, we went through on aggregate as it was 2-2 and in those days an away goal counted double. That rule has only recently been changed but we got the benefit of it then, so Groningen beat Atlético Madrid, who were the hot favourites. It was a great result for us. We had some good players but we didn't have star players like Atlético had. Winning against a team like that is one of the highlights in the history of FC Groningen. It was amazing stuff. I only wish I had gone back to the shop the day after but, unfortunately, we didn't have enough time. I would have loved to have seen the look on that man's face.

After the game when we went back to the hotel, Jan van Dijk, who was our captain, said to everybody that it was time for a party. We all said great, but our manager, Hans Westerhof, who was, remember, at the time quite inexperienced in working with top-level footballers, said that nobody was to go out. He and Van Dijk started to argue about it and almost started a fight, so what Westerhof did was to have all the staff patrolling the whole area of the hotel. Every door was manned and they stayed up guarding them the whole night! I was young and quite fresh at the time so I went back to my room, but some of the older guys were shocked. I mean, how many times does a team like FC Groningen win at Atlético Madrid, with all their stars?

In the next round of the competition we played against the Swiss side Servette. The first game was at home and we won 2-0, and then two weeks later we went to Switzerland for the away game. When we were there, Martin Koeman, the father of Ronald and Erwin, who was the assistant manager at the time, was sitting next to me at the pre-match meal and he started talking to me and said that Servette had made an offer to buy me. That might have been the case but to tell me then at that time? How daft can you be? I was supposed to be focusing on the game and he tells me that! It was terrible timing. Renze de Vries was our chairman and said that Groningen wouldn't sell me because I hadn't been at the club very long and I had signed a three-year deal, so any possible transfer to Servette would not go ahead. Had they sold me it would have been a good piece of business for the club because it turned out that Servette had offered two million guilders.

Then, out of the blue, at least it was to me, Groningen found themselves in trouble. The tax inspectors did an investigation and it was found that they were playing black money to players. The authorities were interviewing every player, asking if they had received any underhand money, and it turned out that there were a couple of players who were involved. I have to say at this point that I was never offered nor did I ask for any dirty money and I didn't even realise what was happening at the time. De Vries was found guilty of embezzlement by the Fiscal Information and Investigation Service for using dirty money to persuade players to join the club, and he stepped down from being chairman. This whole affair had a big effect on FC Groningen. They had to pay a lot of money back to the tax people and they actually came close to bankruptcy.

The second leg in Switzerland ended in a 1-1 draw and we went through 3-1 on aggregate to play Stuttgart in the next round. Stuttgart had a lot of good players. A young Jürgen Klinsmann was their star striker before he moved to Inter Milan and then Monaco, Tottenham and Bayern Munich; Guido Buchwald, the German defender who played many times for their national team, was there; Eike Immel the German international goalkeeper was playing also – they had a really good team.

We started well but then it began to rain and the conditions made playing good football almost impossible. The Germans were physical and we had a few smaller technical players, so they had the upper hand then. They put Srecko Katanec on me to mark me. Katanec was a good player, an international for Yugoslavia at the time. Despite the game being a hard one, two of the most bizarre things I've ever seen on a football pitch happened that day. We lost the game 3-1, and for one of the goals our captain, Jan van Dijk, was trying to play the Stuttgart forwards offside. The problem was that he was standing in Stuttgart's half! He was the last player but was five yards over the halfway line. He stopped playing and raised his hand wanting the referee to stop the game for offside. Of course, the game continued and their player had a free run in on goal with a couple of our other players hopelessly tying to catch him.

The other bizarre incident was when a long-range shot was fired at our goal. It wasn't just long-range, it was stupidly long-range, probably 35 or 40 yards. Because it was raining and so muddy, though, our goalie Jahann Tukker tried to jump but, due to the sticky mud he was in and the rain soaking his boots, he couldn't really get off the ground. The ball just flew over him and into the net. Why was he standing in the mud in the first place? Just move out a little bit to make it easier for yourself to jump and dive! Stuttgart won 3-1 but, really, those two goals should never have been conceded so, who knows, we might have got a better result on a normal day. Two comic goals – unbelievable. For the second leg we went over to Stuttgart and they beat us 2-0 and we were out. In fact, Stuttgart got to the final that year and were beaten 5-4 by Napoli in a really exciting final over two legs.

We had a good team with some good players, we were all friends, and that year we also got to the Dutch Cup Final. We were lucky to beat an amateur team called Harderwijk in one of the early rounds, going through 1-0 with a goal right at the end. Whether that scared us or not I don't know, but from then on we put in some great performances. In the quarter-final we beat Ajax, which was a really good result for us because they had a great team with some great players, internationals all the way through the side. They had Wim Jonk, Jan Wouters, Dennis Bergkamp, Arnold Mühren, Danny Blind, etc. – such a good team. Most times we played them in the league they beat us easily but in the cup game it was one of our best performances of the season and we won 3-0. Then we beat Willem II in the semi-final very easily, 5-1, and we were in the final.

In the final we played PSV Eindhoven, who were also going for the championship. If they did win the league title then they would of course be going into the European Cup the following season, meaning that we would also qualify for Europe as well. We would be through to the Cup Winners' Cup, even if we didn't actually win the cup because Eindhoven obviously couldn't play in two different European competitions. The thing is, Groningen also had to play PSV in the league in the second-last game of the season, with them coming to our ground. They were three points ahead of Ajax so, if they beat us, they would become champions as it was still two points for a win in those days. PSV won the game 2-1 and at the final whistle we weren't overly concerned that we had lost. I mean, we didn't throw the match or anything like that, it's just the way it worked out. They had a really good team. The Brazilian Romário was their centre-forward, what a brilliant player he was; they had Eric Gerets the Belgian defender, who was a terrific player; Wim Kieft, Ronald Koeman, Gerald Vanenburg … in every position they had a top player. It shows how good they were that they were the current European champions at that time. The season before they had beaten Benfica in the final and nobody ever wins the European Cup without being a very good team. They were going through probably the best period in their history. After the game we went into their dressing room and we celebrated together – they because they were champions and us because we had qualified for Europe the following season. There was champagne flowing and we were jumping around together. It was a great time!

Two weeks later we met them again in the cup final and there was a suggestion that the game should be played in Eindhoven instead of at Feyenoord where it was scheduled to be. The final is always played at De Kuip, the stadium of Feyenoord, in Rotterdam, but a request came through to play the final at PSV's stadium. The official reason was that there wasn't expected to be a full house, with the local supporters not being that interested in the game considering that Rotterdam is in the west of Holland and the two competing teams were based nowhere near. Groningen are in the north and Eindhoven are in the south. We had a team meeting about it and the question of money was raised. If we moved the game to Eindhoven in front of 35,000 or 40,000, how much would we make? The answer came back that it would be about 6,000 guilders per player, win or lose. Money aside, I also made the point that I thought we would have a better chance of beating PSV at their own stadium in front of their own supporters. We had done pretty well in our league game there that season; they beat us but only 1-0, and playing at their ground would add a little bit of pressure on them. I thought we would have a better chance there than playing at a neutral ground in front of a lot fewer people. Hans Westerhof, though, was convinced that we would have a better chance against them if we played at Feyenoord, so we voted on it. The result was an easy victory for those who wanted to play at

Feyenoord, about 20 votes against three, or something like that. I went along with it, obviously, but I thought they were all crazy.

Apart from the footballing reasons for my wanting to play the cup final in Eindhoven, if we went there and failed to lift the cup at least we would all earn the 6,000 guilders. I don't want to sound mercenary, but 6,000 guilders was a lot of money back then. I mean, you wouldn't turn down being given that now, but imagine how much it was considering the cost of living in 1989! The equivalent today is about €20,000. But no. Hans Westerhof said we had to go and win the cup in Rotterdam. Okay, that was the vote, so we had to get on with it. When the cup final came around, I hadn't even touched the ball when Romário scored their first goal. The game was completely one-sided, we were played off the park and we lost 4-1. Henny Meijer scored our only goal when we were already three down, and then straight away they went and scored their fourth anyway. There were only 10,000 people watching the game, there was a lousy atmosphere and not only were we given a spanking on the pitch, but we made only 500 guilders, and that was before tax!

As I said, we had a good team at that point but that was it, a good team. We had 11 or 12 good players but when some were out with injuries or whatever the level dropped. Our squad was really quite tight. That's the difference between the top couple of clubs in Holland and the rest of us – at least it was at that time. Eindhoven and Ajax had good squads, whereas the others had good teams. A lot of the Groningen squad were local to the area but PSV could afford to buy in players like Romário from Brazil and Søren Lerby from Denmark, great players who were stars for their country. PSV had also sold Ruud Gullit to AC Milan for £5m, which was a world record transfer fee at that time, so they had all that money to spend on players as well.

During that 1988/89 season there had been an incident that to this day I still don't understand. We had a player called Sixto Rovina, who had joined us at the start of that year from FC Eindhoven. He had been an amateur there and was an international for the Netherlands Antilles. The Antilles had previously played under the name of Curaçao until 1958, even though it had been ten years since the area's name had changed to Netherlands Antilles. In 2010, the Antilles dissolved into two new countries – Sint Maarten and Curaçao again – and three new municipalities – Bonaire, Saba and Sint Eustatius.

Anyway, Sixto Rovina had joined us that season and, although he was retained on amateur status, he would train with us and get his bonuses, and he was one of the boys. Then one Wednesday morning on a day off, I got a telephone call at home from one of the senior players who was at the club in the players' lounge. He told me that Sixto had died the previous evening. He had been playing a match for the second team against VV Hoogezand and suffered a heart attack. All the players were being called into the club.

Everyone gathered at the club, not just the players but the management but the board members as well, and we were talking about what had happened and saying how sorry we were because he was such a nice lad. It seems he had taken a throw-in and just fell forward and that was it. Apparently he'd had some problems with his heart in the past, which we didn't know about. The club really should have known because when they sign a player they have to go through a medical to make sure everything is okay but, because he was an amateur, maybe their tests weren't so stringent, I don't know. That's just a guess.

'Presumably our game at the weekend is going to be called off?' I asked. We were due to play MVV Maastricht.

The chairman said that, no, the game was still on. I couldn't believe it.

'But a team-mate has just died,' I said, 'and now we have to play a match? I'm not going to play until after he has been buried.'

'Yes, but he has to go to Suriname, so it will take some time,' was the argument.

It turned out that because he didn't have a professional contract we would have to carry on. If he was on a contract, then the game would have been postponed. So it seems that it wasn't about being one of the boys, it was all about paperwork. How can paperwork be more important than a human life? Something is seriously wrong with that. How could the KNVB, the Dutch football association, possibly go along with that? They don't feel our grief. One of our team-mates dies on a Tuesday and they expect us to play at the weekend just wearing a black armband? That's ridiculous. I made it clear that I wasn't going to play.

There was a lot of discussion. The board members were saying that if we don't play we will get a fine and maybe even a points deduction. I just couldn't believe that we were even discussing the situation.

'Come on, coach, make a stand,' I said to Hans Westerhof. 'Who cares about the football association and their stupid rule? If they're going to fine us, let them fine us. We need to stick together as a group for Sixto Rovina. We're not going to play, because one of our team-mates has died. It makes no difference if he had a contract or not.'

'Okay,' Westerhof said, 'anybody can make their own decision but we have to play against Maastricht.'

I expected that the other players would have the same reaction as me but, as it turned out, I was alone. Everybody else agreed that it was stupid that we would have to play but also said that we would have to follow the rules. I told them all that they were nutters and that the club had to do something about the situation. How can paperwork and money be more important than a person's life? Why was there no respect being shown to the boy? Why was there no respect being shown to his family?

The next day, Thursday, we had a training session. On the Friday we had another training session and then the bus left Groningen to go to Maastricht that afternoon rather than on the day of the game because Groningen to Maastricht is a 350-kilometre drive, the longest journey to a match we had. We were right up in the north-east corner and Maastricht is on the Belgian border in the far south of the country. I reiterated to Hans Westerhof on the Friday that I wasn't going to play and that I would be driving back home after training. I told him that if he wanted to give me a fine, then give me a fine, but I just felt that I couldn't play. To be fair to him he said that I wouldn't be fined because he had said everybody could make their own decision what to do, but the club insisted that we were to play the match because it was the rules. Before the bus left, he spoke to the players again, asking if there were any others with the same opinion as me. There were a couple of players who spoke up saying they had the same opinion but they still went to the match.

For the record, the match ended in a 3-1 win for Maastricht.

My last year at Groningen was my best year. We had signed Milko Djurovski from Partizan Belgrade, and what a player he was. He had played international football for Yugoslavia and then went on to represent Macedonia. We had played against Belgrade in Europe in the Cup Winners' Cup after qualifying because we were runners-up in the Dutch Cup to Eindhoven. We won at home 4-3 in a tremendous game. We should have beaten them by more but we conceded two poor goals. We created so many chances and really should have won the game easily enough to make the second leg a formality. Djurovski was their star player, the only one that really caused us any major problems, and he scored two of their goals. In Belgrade for the second leg they scored first, Djurovski again, and I scored with ten minutes to go to make it 1-1, so we were again ahead on aggregate and going into the next round. They were then given a corner that wasn't a corner, it should have been a goal kick, and they scored from it to make it 2-1, so once again we were heading out of the competition. For the last few minutes we threw everything at them but just couldn't get that second equaliser. Then in injury time Djurovski scored again for 3-1 and we were out. Over the two legs he had scored four of their seven goals and was the difference between the two teams.

After 29 games we were only two points behind PSV with our next match being away against FC Twente. We smashed them on the pitch, really played well, hardly gave them a touch of the ball but somehow managed to lose 4-2. Even though we had played so well throughout that season and got some really good results, we had never been so dominant in a game as we had then. How we didn't get an easy victory that day I really don't know. The next day PSV played their game and they lost as well, so if we had beaten Twente we would have been on top of the league.

After that we had nine matches left but only managed to win four of them. The following game after Twente was against Feyenoord and everything started to go wrong. We picked up injuries, we were awarded red cards, the players who were drafted into the matchday squad just weren't quite good enough, and we finished the season in third place behind PSV and Ajax. That was the closest I ever came to being a league champion. I was denied my medal by the depth of squad or, more accurately, by the lack of the depth of squad. It was still a great season for the club but it could have been a brilliant one.

That whole year the club was thinking who would be out of contract in the summer that they could make some money from, and my three years were up so they put me on the transfer list.

They wanted to keep Djurovski and Meijer but because of the financial situation they wanted to earn half a million guilders, which was a lot of money in those days. It was in Holland, anyway. So they got Ton van Dalen involved. Van Dalen had done a lot of work with Aberdeen previously, he knew Alex Smith and had helped with the transfer of Theo Snelders to Scotland from FC Twente. I think he might have also helped out with Hans Gillhaus as well. He knew all the Dutch players and had contacts in Britain.

After a while I heard that Nottingham Forest were interested in taking me over to England. They had previously had a couple of Dutch players – Hans van Breukelen and Jonny Metgod – who had both been a big success there. My wife was heavily pregnant at the time that they registered their interest and sent their scout over to watch Groningen play PSV in the January of 1991. As it turned out I didn't play in that game because my son was born, so I missed the chance to play in front of the representatives of Nottingham Forest.

The following Wednesday we had a cup game against Ajax and I arrived back at Groningen to train with the squad on the Tuesday, the day before the match. When we got to Amsterdam, Hans Westerhof told me I wouldn't be playing. I couldn't really understand it and was quite angry at him because we knew the Nottingham Forest people would be there to watch me. I asked him why he had made that decision, knowing that the scouts would be there. They had made a special trip over to see me because they knew a couple of Scottish teams were also interested and they wanted to make sure they got there first. Westerhof said I wouldn't be playing because the circumstances meant that I had missed a couple of training sessions. We had a conversation about it but that was his decision. I didn't like it but I had to accept it. I then found out from hearing the sports news on the radio that Stefan Pettersson, Ajax's Swedish striker, would be playing even though his wife had also delivered a baby the previous weekend. So, when Westerhof had told the media that Ten Caat wouldn't be playing, the Ajax manager Leo Beenhakker had said that Pettersson would be. This reignited my anger. There was steam coming out of my ears. I went straight back to speak with the manager again.

'What is happening here?' I demanded, 'you're running my career now.'

He wouldn't budge. 'You're not playing. If Beenhakker wants to pick Pettersson that's his business, and it's also my business who I choose for my team. You're on the bench.'

'Well in that case you're going to lose the match.' That was my final word.

When the game came round, just before half-time one of the players, Harris Huizingh, went down injured so Westerhof told me to warm up. Okay, it wasn't the ideal situation that I had wanted but at least I would get a chance to show Forest what I could do. During the half-time break the physio came up to me and said, 'I'm sorry, Theo, he will be fit enough to carry on.'

'Oh, come on,' I said, 'don't joke with me. The manager said I was going on and I've been warming up. Tell the manager he can choose now. Either he's going to play me now or I'm going to take a shower.'

Westerhof came over and confirmed the diagnosis. 'Well, Theo, it turns out that he is okay, so he can carry on.'

'Have you spoken with the physio?' I asked. 'Because I told him that if you're not going to play me now I'm going to take a shower.'

He looked at me, went back over to the physio and ended up making the substitution. I played in the second half. Had he said to me, 'Okay, get in the shower, then,' that's exactly what I would have done. I was fed up because I wasn't playing and I was fed up because I knew that Nottingham Forest were watching me, or at least wanting to watch me. We lost the game 3-1 but at least I got on for a while.

A couple of weeks later we had to play Ajax again, this time in the league, and this time I was back in and played the full game. We went to Amsterdam and came away with a 1-1 draw. I said to Westerhof after the game, 'You see? That's what happens when you play against Ajax and you play Theo ten Caat. You don't lose!'

I was making a joke of it but really I was only half-joking. I was still angry that I had missed the chance to sign for Nottingham Forest and play under the legendary Brian Clough. How the two of us would have got on together is anybody's guess but I'm sure it would have been a lot of fun finding out. I understand that they couldn't take a chance on buying me having only seen me play one half of one game. I fully understand that.

Then towards the end of the season, with my contract running out, Aberdeen came in for me. I knew a bit about Aberdeen from having watched them in Europe and winning the Cup Winners' Cup in 1983. They played some really good football, with players like Willie Miller, Alex McLeish and Gordon Strachan and, of course, the manager was Alex Ferguson, and it was good to watch them. Then when Theo Snelders signed for them I kept an eye on what they were doing, so I always knew something about the club. When I heard about their interest they weren't just a team in Scotland who wanted to sign me, they were Aberdeen Football Club, so as soon as I knew I had a chance of joining them, my mind was virtually made up. There was a bit of noise that Dundee United might make a bid for me but, to be completely honest, I didn't really fancy that much anyway, especially if my other option was Aberdeen.

This was shortly before the Bosman rule came in regarding transfers. When a player's contract ran out back then he was still owned by the club and couldn't just pick and choose where he wanted to play next as they can now. The whole law change came about through the Belgian player Jean-Marc Bosman. He was playing for Liège in Belgium, and when his contract finished he wanted to move to Dunkerque in France. Liège asked for a certain transfer fee to be paid, which Dunkerque refused to meet or couldn't afford, and the move didn't go ahead. At that time Liège were still entitled to ask for a transfer fee even though, technically, because the player's contract had ended, he should have been a free agent. In no other business is a person still owned by their company when their contract has finished. For example, if I work in an accountancy company and I'm contracted to do a certain job for three years, when the three years ends and my contract is complete, then I no longer work for the company, I can go wherever I want. That's how it is in any walk of life but it wasn't like that in football. Not only was Jean-Marc Bosman denied his transfer to France but, as he was no longer a member of the first-team squad of Liège, his wages were also cut. He believed that his freedom of movement had been impeded and he took his case to the European Court of Justice. The court agreed with him and he won the case. Now, because of Jean-Marc Bosman, when a player's contract is over he can move where he wants. Not only that, but the ruling also stopped each country's football league from having a rule that you could only have a certain number of foreign players in your squad. Actually, the first British player to benefit from the Bosman ruling was Paul Kane when he moved from Aberdeen to Viking Stavanger in Norway.

Anyway, when I heard that Aberdeen wanted to sign me I was quite excited. Even though I knew a bit about them, I never thought I would have a chance to play for them. If the move happened today it would be a free transfer but Groningen received the money they wanted, I became an Aberdeen player and everyone was happy.

Arriving in Aberdeen

Oh my goodness, what a start. Forget Lanarkshire,
I thought I was in Hell!

MY WIFE and I took a flight from Amsterdam to Aberdeen full of excitement for our new adventure. This time we were not only moving to a new club but moving to a new country as well. The United Kingdom was the home of football, it was where it all began, the rules of the game were written there. Scotland vs England was the first-ever international match in 1872. The FA Cup is the oldest football competition in the world, the Scottish Cup the second and only by a couple of years.

The first we saw of Aberdeen was that it was raining. Not only was it raining but it was also windy and it was grey. That was our first impression but it turns out that Aberdeen is a beautiful city, at least from our point of view. We got a taxi from the airport to the hotel that we were booked into. Rod Stewart was playing on the radio, and we had a meeting and a meal that evening with the board members. This was an experience all of its own. I could speak English but it seems I couldn't speak Scottish. The accent was just something else. They were talking, talking, talking, and it was so fast. I could speak decent English at that time but I couldn't understand a word they were saying! They kept saying 'wee' – this was 'wee', that was 'wee'. What is this 'wee'? Apparently, they meant a 'little'. Exciting though it is, it's also a challenge moving from country to country and those kinds of little things made it harder still. Then on the second day we had the contract negotiations, came to an agreement and I was an Aberdeen player.

Alex Smith, the manager of Aberdeen at the time, is one of the nicest guys I've ever met in football. He was a father figure to me. He really helped me settle into my new life. Jocky Scott was there as well as the assistant manager and Drew Jarvie was the trainer. Drew Jarvie is a really nice guy too, and he helped me a lot.

The first thing I did as an Aberdeen player was to go to Bermuda. Not to escape the wind and rain for some Caribbean sun, but the team went there on a pre-season trip. For me it was too hot. I had just about adjusted to the Scottish weather and now here we were in Bermuda, with the temperature in Celsius being the temperature in Fahrenheit back in Scotland! Before we arrived in Bermuda we made a stopover in New York. We came into the airport and they warned us we were in a dangerous area and we weren't allowed to leave the hotel, so that wasn't too good for a start. I was sharing a room with Theo Snelders and we then found out that our toilet didn't work! We stayed awake almost the whole night because the guy was in our room trying to fix the toilet. It took hours. The problem was that when we went to the toilet it didn't flush away. The level just rose, it went up and up and over the edge, all over the floor. They eventually fixed it but it took hours and we hardly got any sleep at all that night.

That was New York but then I got sick in Bermuda. I was eating chicken, threw up and went down with a fever. The team had a couple of friendly games scheduled in over there but I couldn't train much and I couldn't play much. All I could really do was a bit of swimming and a bit of snorkelling, but even that wasn't too great as I couldn't get my head under the water. What a great start for my being an Aberdeen player! I was hoping to make a really good first impression, of course, but here I was straight on the sick list.

Those things aside, it was good to get to know the players and the staff and to see how things were organised. The team went on a boat trip, which was nice, but it turned out that David Winnie was afraid of the water. He went in okay, but as soon as he touched a fish he started screaming and wanted to get straight back in the boat again. Of course, the whole team were on his back about it but it was all good fun and good humour.

We play two games over there but, because I had been ill, I wasn't able to be involved much. I made a brief substitute appearance in the second game but that was all. The team did well, though, and we recorded a 2-0 and a 4-0 victory and that was that, trip over. After that it wasn't straight back to Scotland for me as it was for the other boys. My wife and I had a few things to arrange back in Holland for our move to Scotland so my rather convoluted route back was Bermuda to

New York, from New York to Manchester, from Manchester to Aberdeen, from Aberdeen to Amsterdam and then finally back from Amsterdam to Aberdeen. When I finally arrived back in Aberdeen it was straight into pre-season training to prepare for the 1991/92 season.

We had a friendly match against Raith Rovers and then went to Elgin City to play in a testimonial game for Chris Slavin, which we won 7-0. At that time Elgin were in the Highland League. I have to say the scenery up there was brilliant, really beautiful. I really like the old-type stadiums, too. Some people might look at them and think that they need upgrading or modernising, but I like the feel of the older grounds, they have a certain feeling about them that's the heart and soul of football. In Holland everything is neat and tidy and shiny, but it wasn't so much the case in Scotland, which I liked. It's more real. It's just the little things like the open stands, the click of the turnstiles and lining up to buy a pie! During my time at Aberdeen, Raith Rovers was one of my favourite away grounds to visit. It was a nice ground plus there was lots of lovely scenery around and the train track. I was always hoping that in the cup we would get an away draw at Raith.

The last warm-up game before the season kicked off was the tall ships game against Manchester United. This was certainly an interesting one. There was a tall ships race going on at the time, with Aberdeen harbour being one of the venues used, with many ships taking part. We had a friendly with Man United at the same time and they brought up a decent team – there was Peter Schmeichel in goal, players like Dennis Irwin, Mark Hughes, Paul Ince, Brian McClair and so on.

This was my first serious game for Aberdeen, but we never talked about tactics! In Holland we spent a lot of time considering the tactical aspect of the game, team organisation and how to play. Do we use a 4-3-3 formation or a 4-4-2 or try something else? There were a lot of systems and every player knew what to do in every part of the pitch. I thought we would play the same strategy as we did in Holland. If you want to press, you press trying to get the ball with the midfield going forward and the defence following them forward. But that wasn't the case. They just said, 'Okay, you're going to play in that position,' but never went too deeply into what 'that position' demanded. We weren't told how we were to interrupt the build-up of the opponents, just that 'the back four stay in a line'.

So, we played 4-4-2 with the four midfielders in a line. I was playing wide on the left with the rest of the midfield being made up of Peter van de Ven, Jim Bett and Brian Grant. In the defence we had Stewart McKimmie, Stephen Wright, Alex McLeish and Robert Connor, in front of Theo Snelders, with Eoin Jess and Hans Gillhaus playing up front. When the match got underway I started to play exactly as I had been used to playing for Groningen. That was how I had always played and it's how I was playing when Aberdeen decided to buy me, so why would I be any different? In Holland we always push on to put pressure on the opposition, so against United I pushed forward to put the pressure on Irwin, who was the United full-back on my side. The problem was that Robert Connor wouldn't push on to cover the midfielder that I had left. That meant that, as I was pushing forward, there was a big space behind me and their midfielder was always getting the ball. This happened a few times in the first half. My way of thinking was that if I'm pushing forward, he has to push forward too. Then the centre-half moves to the left and we switch to playing three at the back for the moment against their two strikers. That would make sense to me. Or Grantie has to push forward and we all go in a line, but they all stayed in the same area.

After a while I said to Robert Connor, our left-back, 'Come on, you have to push forward, we have to go in a line. If I go ten yards here you go ten yards here, if I go ten yards there you go ten yards there. If the ball goes backwards, we go backwards; if the ball goes forwards, we go forwards.'

'No, no, no, I can't push forward,' he said.

I couldn't understand why. 'You have to push forward, you're in empty space, you don't have an opponent.'

'It's a slightly different game in Scotland,' he told me. 'If I push forward the strikers will go into the wide areas, but our centre-halves want to stay in the middle, they want to stay in the box, that's what they're interested in. If their strikers go wide I have to pick them up.'

I still didn't get it. If you stay in the box it means you're nearer your goal, so stay out of the box.

Alex Smith said to me later, 'There are a couple of things you have to learn. Get the ball in the angles and over the top.'

'What's that?' I asked him. 'What are these angles?'

He said, 'A ball over the top is a long one for the centre-forward and the angles are when it's out at the corner.'

Okay, that's fine by me if they wanted to play like that, but they should have told me before. In Holland every game is technical and tactical. If we want to press forward, every part of the training session beforehand is about pushing forward, so I had to adjust on that matter.

The pace of the game in Scotland is very different as well. Not only the pace of the ball being played, but also the pace of the players. Sometimes it looked like they were just running around in circles. For example, if we hit a long ball up to Scott Booth he would start running after it, even if he knew the ball was going over the goal line. I thought, *If you can see the ball is too hard and going too far, stop running.* What the manager always said was, 'You have to make a run and make a good ball from a bad ball.'

The goalkeeper John Burridge, who joined us for a while a couple of years later, also tried to explain it to me in a simple way. He said, 'You play the ball over the top at an angle into the corner and then you make a challenge, which will always result in one of two outcomes. The first one is that the ball goes out for a throw to your opponent and you just block it there. The second outcome is that we get a throw and then try to get the ball into the box and have a shot. That in itself then creates even more options. Either the goalie saves it, he touches it away and it goes for a corner or you score a goal. If you get a corner, you throw everybody into the box and try to make a chance out of it.'

I understood what he meant but there was nothing about midfield play or different combinations or anything like that. If you want to surprise your opponent you have to play in different styles and with different tempos. Start off slow, increase the tempo, slow it down again, things like this. You play through the first man, the second man, you come over to the wide areas, moving the ball from one side to the other side. That way it's more about keeping the ball and not losing it again. The way that I was now being asked to play was very different to Dutch football. I was playing passes, that's how I had learned to play.

I remember I also had an exchange with Jocky Scott about it. He was giving me stick because I was playing the little passes in the midfield, but they couldn't handle the quickness of the precision game, the really small passes. If it went big, they could handle it but the small passes, the tiki-taka like Barcelona play, they couldn't handle it. Jocky was always saying, 'Hey, Theo, always those wee passes.' I told him, 'Is it my fault that he keeps losing the ball? No, it's his fault, don't blame me. If he can't handle the wee passes he should be out of the team!'

That match with United finished 1-1 and they beat us in a penalty shoot-out to decide the winner. I scored our goal that day and afterwards everyone was talking about me: 'Look at the new player, our new Dutchman, he scored a beautiful goal.' With that sort of talk going around I didn't really care about the tactics, anyway!

The 1991/92 season kicked off and our first match was away at Airdrie, my proper debut for Aberdeen. Oh my goodness, what a start. Forget Lanarkshire, I thought I was in Hell! We went down there to Broomfield Park (unfortunately it got sold a couple of seasons later and the club moved elsewhere) and I thought it was a beautiful stadium – quite old but really nice, just the sort that I've already said that I like – and I was really looking forward to it. When the game started, though, what was going on? We had been playing for about 20 minutes and the ball was in the air most of the time, there wasn't much happening on the grass. It was all kick and rush, more of a battle than a game, and I was thinking, *What the heck is this?*

The lads told me this is the Scottish football game. It's not all just against Celtic and Rangers, you have to adjust to this sort of game. I thought, *Wow, this is going to be three beautiful years, then!* After about 20 or 25 minutes, with me trying to play my Dutch style of football, one of their guys came and just clattered into me. I think there's a photo of it somewhere where they've got three shots. The first is me being kicked, the second is me bending over in the air and the third is me dropping on to the floor. I made a somersault and my ankle was swollen as big as a melon, so I had to go off. I went with David Wylie, the physio, back to the changing room and I was sitting there with ice on my ankle. At half-time Jocky Scott went mental at me! He gave me a hairdryer, shouting at me that I had to adjust to the Scottish game.

'What's this, are you insane? The guy kicked me! I can't do anything about that, can I?' I said, pointing down at my ankle. 'I didn't kick myself, he kicked me. What can I do?'

'You had better pay attention and get tackles in,' he shouted, telling me that I had to adjust to the Scottish game sooner rather than later or he would personally send me back home in a plane.

What? If that's what you wanted you should have left me in Holland. I'm a football player. If you just wanted somebody who liked running around and kicking people you should have taken somebody else. I didn't come over here to fight with Jocky Scott. I was hacked off. You can't behave towards players like that. What he was trying to do was imitate Alex Ferguson. I didn't know that at the time but that's what he was doing, or at least trying to do. When the players left the dressing room, Alex Smith, who I always got on with, gave me a hug. Because of that tackle, if you can call it a tackle, I was out for four weeks.

We actually started the season really well. After my shocker against Airdrie and being out for a while after that, I was back in the team for a trip to Motherwell, which we won 1-0, and then we had to play Copenhagen in the UEFA Cup. The first leg was at Pittodrie and, even though we played a good game that evening, we somehow managed to lose the match. We missed so many chances and they scored in the last couple of minutes to take away a 1-0 win. It was a terrible result for us.

Two days after that game Jocky Scott decided to leave Aberdeen to take up the manager's position at Dunfermline. They had parted company with their previous manager Ian

Munro and Jocky took up the challenge of being boss in his own right rather than part of a management trio with Alex and Drew. The ironic thing here being that six weeks after he had threatened to see me off back to Holland in a plane, it was me who had seen him off as he sped away down the A90!

Before the second leg with Copenhagen we went to Ibrox to play Rangers, a match that I thoroughly enjoyed. I was one of the best players on the pitch. We won 2-0 and I set up Eoin Jess for the first goal before Brian Grant made the game safe. From the high of our victory there we went to Denmark, lost 2-0 and that was it. That was, basically, my European adventure with Aberdeen.

By that time in the season the way we played in midfield had settled down a bit from my first experience during pre-season and had become a bit more similar to what I had been used to back home with the passing interchanging, the combinations and playing forward. There was myself, Jim Bett, Brian Grant and Paul Mason, who were all fairly similar in the way we liked to play the game. Paul had played in Holland with Groningen and Jim had played in Belgium with Lokeren, so the three of us had a European style. Grantie was more a Scottish style, of course, but he could fit in well with us. I think we had a really good midfield department then.

One or two new players began to arrive who, in my opinion, didn't really fit into the same sort of midfield pattern that we had. Paul Kane was brought in from Oldham in England after spending some time at Hibernian. Paul was a good guy, don't get me wrong, but he just had a different playing style. So then we had Grantie and Kane, two typical Scottish players, and two European-style players in the midfield, and the balance just changed. We now had two fighters in there and, if you fight too much, you forget to play football. Then it becomes a circular thing because you have to play football to avoid a fight. If there are too many heavy challenges going in and trying to get one up on your direct opponent, you then start to forget that the important part is to control the midfield. The way to do that is by keeping possession of the ball because then you can attack, and if you don't do that then you have to defend. It sounds obvious but it does make a difference. The further you go from your own goal towards the goal of your opponents the easier it is to defend. With the new players that had come in, and I mean absolutely no disrespect to any of them, our tactics and the way we played changed subtly and we were more on the back foot instead of the front foot. In my opinion, that's when the team's fortunes begin to change a little. I'm not blaming the ones who came into the team, it's just the way the tactics changed and then it wasn't really the balance that we'd had previously. There's a phrase that goes 'attack wins games, defence wins championships', which is all very well but you have to actually win the games first.

Another big factor, I think, in the team's inconsistency that season was the injury to Alex McLeish. He was out for a long while, which was a big blow for us because he was the main man. When Alex wasn't in the team, the team became weaker. That's not a slight on any of the players who took over from him but if you take Alex McLeish out of any team, pretty much any team in the world at that time, they would have been weaker. Gary Smith came in, who was only a young boy at the time, and he did well, but Alex McLeish's boots are big boots to fill.

In February we were beaten 1-0 at home by Hibernian and there was a bit of unrest among the supporters outside the main gate after the game. On the Monday we got a call and all had a meeting where we were told that Alex had been sacked. I was really sad. In that game against Hibs I had three decent chances to score and missed them all. Had one of them gone in, or two of them maybe, it would have been a different story, I don't know. Or maybe it would have just held off until the next game or the next loss. When it was announced that Willie Miller would be the new manager I wasn't surprised because he had been around the club for a little while. He had been appointed as a coach for the reserve team and was on the bench when we played the first leg against Copenhagen at Pittodrie. We lost the game 1-0 and there were a few shouts from the crowd: 'There's only one Willie Miller,' and it was that moment, in my opinion, that the crowd wanted Willie back as manager and Alex Smith out. As I've already said, I got on really well with Alex and had a lot of respect for him, and hearing of his dismissal was a sad day for me, especially as it was only half a season since I had joined as one of his signings.

So Willie came in and immediately the fans were on his side. His first game was at Ibrox of all places, and we got a good

0-0 draw. He started to make some changes to the squad, his first signing being Mixu Paatelainen. When Mixu arrived, Jim Bett came up to me and we had a conversation of which, at the time, I didn't really get the full meaning.

'This might be interesting,' he said to me.

'Okay,' I said, 'what does that mean?'

'He's from Dundee United and he's a striker.'

I didn't really get where he was going with this so I asked him what he meant.

'Theo,' he said, 'we won't be getting any balls to our feet again. When Mixu is in the team just listen and you will hear something.'

Obviously, this got me interested and I thought about what he had said during the days after. Then the time came for Mixu to play his first game. We were away at Dunfermline, who were now Jocky Scott's team, and I understood what Jim had meant.

'Hit Mixu ... hit Mixu,' were the shouts from the bench. And it was like that ever afterwards. Jim and I always made jokes about it. When the back four got the ball we would tell them, 'Hit Mixu.' It got to the point where we didn't even ask for the ball anymore. It was so predictable for the rest of that year, it drove me crazy. To be fair to him, Mixu was brilliant in the air and I have nothing against him personally, not at all. We had a good relationship. We used to go clay pigeon shooting together, he was really good at that. We also used to play snooker together. He was good at snooker and I was rubbish so maybe that's why he always wanted to play me, so that he would always win. On the football pitch, though, Jim was right. He knew exactly what tactics we would start to play with Mixu in the team.

'We've got no chance of playing football now,' Jim told me. 'We just have to battle now.'

I said, 'Jim, I'm not so good at that, it isn't my game. I have to play football. I need to get the ball and be on the move. My game is more the combination game with the wee little passes. If I'm now only going to be battling for the second ball, I'll be useless. I won't have a future here anymore.'

We used to come into training on the Monday after a game and have a joke with each other that we needed a good massage on our necks. Our legs were good because we had hardly used them but our necks were stiff from continually looking upwards as the ball was flying over our heads towards our centre-forward.

I was a football player and I wanted to play football the way I played football. Midfielders need to be midfielders, combining with one another, passing and moving, box to box, ten goals a season and ten other assists. That's presumably why Alex Smith signed me in the first place. The way we played with him was a bit more continental. Now with him gone, things seemed to be going in a bit of a different direction.

Then, one morning, there was an article in one of the papers when Willie had been in charge for a little while with pictures of the Dutch players and the big headline: 'Out!'

That winter proved that the papers had it correct. There were five of us at the club when the season ended. Hans Gillhaus was out of favour and didn't play for Aberdeen again. He eventually moved back to Holland with Vitesse Arnhem, although his transfer took an awfully long time to go through, almost the whole of the following season. Willem van der Ark went to Utrecht and Peter van de Ven was sold to Hearts. That left me and Theo Snelders. I was now also out of favour, meaning that Theo Snelders was suddenly the only Dutchman who would be regularly in the team. How things had changed in the space of just one season.

Mr Aberdeen, Mr Celtic and the Longest Warm-Up in Football History

Lee Richardson was the other sub and he was laughing at me and waving at me as he went in for half-time, leaving me out there on my own.

THE GAME before the League Cup semi-final match against Celtic in 1992 was possibly one of my best performances in an Aberdeen shirt. We were playing against Partick Thistle at Pittodrie and we won the game easily. It finished 2-0 that day but it could easily have been four, five or even six, that's how dominant we were. We had absolute control of the midfield, we destroyed them. With about 30 minutes of the game to go, there was a bit of activity on the sidelines as Willie was making a substitution. I looked over to see who was getting hooked and saw my number go up. He was putting on Lee Richardson in my place. I was disappointed to go off, considering how well the game was going, and couldn't understand the decision. Jim Bett spoke to me about it after.

'Just understand this, Theo,' he said, 'this has nothing to do with today's game, it has everything to do with Wednesday's game. Roy Aitken will be playing against his old team and you're out.'

I didn't fully understand what he meant at the time, but he knew what was going on.

Afterwards Willie said a few things about the game, nothing too deep and meaningful, just 'well done lads', that sort of thing, which was fair enough. He said we would have a training session on Sunday, Monday and Tuesday and then Wednesday was the semi-final. So we trained on the Sunday, just a normal training session, but then afterwards, as we were getting changed, Jim said to me, 'Do you see what's happening here?'

'What do you mean?' I asked.

'On Saturday you played well, took the game to Partick, made things happen and he took you off. Why do you think he took you off?'

I said, 'I don't know, I haven't a clue.'

'You know what he's going to do now … Mr Celtic, his friend from the national team. You're not playing on Wednesday, Aitken will be in.'

I said, 'Oh, come on, I played probably one of my best games to date.'

If that was indeed going to be the case, then for me it would be a bit of a problem. If I was going to be dropped, not just for Roy Aitken but for anybody, I would need an explanation from Willie before the game. As I've said, I was having a really good game and feeling great before being substituted, so if I wasn't going to be picked for the semi-final then I don't really see what else I could have done to show I should be in the starting XI. We trained on Sunday and nothing happened by way of an explanation. We trained on Monday and nothing happened by way of an explanation. It was in my head, of course, but I didn't say anything. Of course I wanted to play at Hampden, it was a big game, a cup semi-final is a big occasion, but I didn't say anything to Willie. Maybe Jim had got it wrong after all. Maybe I was going to play after all, that's why nothing had been said.

On the Tuesday we had another training session and then we all had lunch together before getting on the bus to go down to Glasgow. When we arrived we had dinner, and when the time came to go to bed, Willie still hadn't said anything. We had a light training session on the Wednesday morning, nothing too strenuous, due to the match being that evening, and then we had a team talk. The moment of truth.

'This is our squad, these are our subs,' Willie told us all, and that was that. Sure enough, Roy Aitken was in the team in my place. Mr Celtic was playing against his former team. In normal circumstances I would have been stunned but this time I already knew I was to be on the bench, I was prepared for it. Jim Bett certainly knew what he was talking about and he was right. I was just expecting that Willie Miller would have a little word with me beforehand about why I wouldn't be playing, whether it was a tactical decision or whatever. That would have been nice. That's what managers in Holland do, they talk to their players. They let them know their thoughts, they give reasons. Even if you don't agree with what they say, you at least respect their decisions because you know why they've made them. In the games I had been playing in during that season leading up to that point, I thought I had done pretty well, so I was expecting a bit of an explanation. I don't think that's unreasonable. Unfortunately, Willie had a different opinion and didn't say anything. Nothing. He didn't even acknowledge that I might have been disappointed by his decision.

It was obvious that nothing would be forthcoming so I decided to just go and ask him after the team meeting, because by now I was annoyed. Honesty is one of the key words for a manager towards his players. If a player feels that the manager is not honest with him anymore then the trust has gone and the relationship has gone, and that's no good for anyone. I didn't want to wait until Hampden, that wouldn't have been fair or good for the team, so I spoke with him at the team hotel. We sat down together and I really wanted to get things straight with him.

'Willie, you're entitled to make any decision you want because you're the manager and it's your team,' I said. 'I was one of the best players on Saturday so why am I not playing today? I already knew something was happening because you took me off against Partick, but you've had four days since then. Why have you not said anything to me? Just a small word would have done. You could have said to me: "Theo, you had a good game against Partick but I want Roy Aiken to play against Celtic." Do you not agree that would have been normal? But you've said nothing and brought in Roy Aitken, who is no good anymore, he's no better than me. He has been on the bench for a while, has recently been out with an injury, and you're taking a chance on this player in a cup semi-final. It has nothing to do with trying to win the game now, this feels like a personal issue. If choosing Roy Aitken to play for Aberdeen against Celtic in a semi-final is your choice, then okay, it's your choice, you're allowed to make that choice. It doesn't make sense to me, probably doesn't make sense to anybody, but if that's your choice, then it's your choice, but you could have explained it to me, because this makes no sense.'

Willie listened to me, said that I was entitled to my opinion but that he made the decision to play Roy in the best interests of the team in a one-off match. The thing is, I was a better player at that time than Roy. I have respect for him for all that he achieved at Celtic, nobody could argue against that, but at this time his best days were behind him and I was in a good run of form. It now came down to Willie having a straight choice between Roy Aitken and Theo ten Caat. Aitken was too slow, couldn't run anymore, couldn't pass, it was right at the end of his playing career. In contrast I was in my top years. Football-wise it didn't make sense and because of this, as a football player, it was really hard for me to accept and I felt let down not to play the semi-final at Hampden Park in front of 60,000 people. It just didn't make sense to me and seemed like it was somehow a personal matter. I could have understood, or at least tried to understand, his reasons had he sat down with me in the days leading up to the game. Sometimes players are allowed to ask for an explanation for why they're not playing. Not always, but sometimes they are and I felt that a cup semi-final is certainly one of those times.

When we got to Hampden Park I was still fed up about the whole situation. All the players went out on to the pitch to have a look round, but being out there made me feel even worse. We went back into the dressing room to get changed, all the players who made up the starting line-up, including Roy Aitken, and the substitutes as well. I got my kit on but I didn't put on my football boots. The players went out to warm up and soak in the pre-match atmosphere but I stayed in, just walking around in the dressing room with my slippers on. I knew that Willie was going to go mad at me. All the boys were warming up, waving and talking with the crowd, and the whole situation had just got to me so much. At that point I didn't care about going out, I didn't care about the atmosphere, the music, etc., and was just waiting for the time when the match would begin so I could go out and sit on the bench for 90 minutes.

Eventually Willie came up to me. 'Theo,' he said, 'why aren't you going out with the boys for a warm-up?'

'Warm-up?' I challenged. 'We never do a warm-up. The only thing we do is stand in the corner with a ball and do a four against one, laughing and joking. That's not a warm-up, that's nothing. I'm not going out, I'm too disappointed.'

Then he said, 'What if you have to come on after two minutes?'

'Even if I do it doesn't make any difference whether I'm standing in the corner kicking a ball a few yards or sitting here in the dressing room,' I answered. 'They're not doing a proper warm-up and I'm not doing a warm-up. I'm staying in here.'

I was expecting a big argument but he didn't say anything. He just walked away, steam coming out of his ears. I followed him out when the game started. After two minutes – the theoretical two minutes he had mentioned earlier – Willie said to me that he wanted me to warm up. Nobody had actually got injured or anything, he was just making his point. Okay, no problem, I started to warm up, I thought for a few minutes, and then he would call me back to sit down again, point proven. But no. The warm-up went on and on. Five minutes, ten minutes, in fact for the whole of the first 45 minutes! Even at half-time I had to carry on with the warm-up. I asked him if I had to go into the dressing room with everybody else and he said, 'No, you carry on with what you're doing.'

Lee Richardson was the other sub and he was laughing at me and waving at me as he went in for half-time, leaving me out there on my own. All the fans as well, they were waving and shouting things at me and I was waving back. I was there just jogging around and waving to the fans. I don't even know if I was waving to the Aberdeen fans or the Celtic fans. Then the boys came back out for the second half, Lee Richardson sat back down on the bench, the coaching staff came out and the game restarted. I hardly saw any of the match because most of the time I had my back towards the pitch doing stretching exercises. The whole second half went by with me still warming up! When the game finished I just went in with everybody else, took a shower, and life goes on.

Thinking about it now, what Willie did was brilliant, actually. From his point of view, it was brilliant, and he was quite right to do so. I respect him for doing it. It was a great thing for a manager to do to a player who was acting like that. Truly, when I think about that situation and what happened, it was brilliant. He had to understand my emotions but, on my part, I had to control my emotions and should have been a good boy in difficult times, which I wasn't. I was a bad boy in difficult times. Now I do respect him for what he did, for asking me to start warming up after two minutes. It actually makes me laugh.

We won the game 1-0, Eoin Jess scoring the goal, and we were in the cup final. I knew I had no chance of playing in the final and I didn't. We played against Rangers back at Hampden and went behind early on when Stuart McCall jumped on a defensive error. Duncan Shearer equalised with a great goal, thumping it in on the turn, and the game went into extra time. As it turned out, Rangers won in really unfortunate circumstances. There was a cross from the left towards Mark Hateley at the back post. He was a big, tall, old-fashioned centre-forward, really good in the air. As the ball came in towards him, our centre-back Gary Smith had to throw himself at the cross to intercept it. He got there before it reached Hateley but sadly for him the ball went into his own net, with Theo Snelders not standing a chance of keeping it out. Had it been up the other end it would have been a brilliant diving-header goal, right into the bottom corner. We can't blame him for it, he absolutely had to make the challenge otherwise the ball would have landed nicely for Hateley and he would have scored but, unluckily for Smith, it goes down as his own goal. Roy Aitken played in the game, of course, but he had to go off midway through the first half due to an injury and was replaced by Lee Richardson.

Some of the players could see what was going on throughout this whole period, with me being dropped from the team and Willie and Roy being big mates. A few of the boys were on my side and could understand my situation but a lot of the team were Willie Miller's players as well. Drew Jarvie was still there on the coaching team and he was on my side. He told me he could understand why I felt the way I did about what was happening, and I also had friends in Jim Bett, David Winnie, Stewart McKimmie, Theo Snelders, all those boys. Sometimes I would have talks with Brian Irvine and he was really good with me. 'Keep your pride,' he would tell me, 'whatever happens make sure you keep your pride.' And he was right. He was always kind to me. Brian is a brilliant guy. Honestly, he's too nice for this world. If you compare Brian Irvine with me … he's the nicest guy in the world. I can be nice, too, but I can also be a pain. If I feel misjudged or somebody is saying things against me or doing me a disservice, something happens to me, it boils up inside me and I just have to defend myself. Brian is completely different, he's so honest and so pure and I think he's one of the nicest people on Earth. He would say to me after training sessions when I was having a hard time, and he probably can't remember this but I remember, he would say to me, 'Remember your pride. They can take anything away from you but they can't take your pride.' And it's true.

So those boys helped me a lot, while some of the others were siding with Willie Miller. They were his signings so naturally they just got on with it. It's not that I had a bad relationship with any of these ones or anything, but they didn't really care about what was happening between Willie and I. I suppose that's only natural; they were looking out for their place in the squad. They would have had that same feeling for Willie that I had towards Alex Smith. They were his players so of course there would be that loyalty to him. Basically, the boys who were there when I started with Alex were good for me and trying to help me in this silly situation. And it was a silly situation, really.

Willie is Mr Aberdeen but, football-wise, I can only presume that he didn't like my type of player, the way I played the game. That, by the way, is fine. Every manager has his own style. I'm a coach now and I'm the same, I like the game to be played in a certain way. The thing is, though, I would never take anything personally against the other person. If a player can't change their style of play to the way I want, then he finds himself on the bench, that's how it goes. In my case at Aberdeen, though, there are a couple of things that I can't really understand. I was technically one of the best players and mentally I was strong, so I thought I should be in the team.

Having said that, I can also understand why Willie didn't choose me, because the Scottish game at that time was very hard, very physical, and Willie wanted to have battles on the field and that wasn't how I played. To be fair, they did play some really good games without me as well. They made it to a cup final and finished second in the league. The problem for me personally was that he wanted to play a different kind of football to how Alex Smith played, so he brought in some different players. He recruited Duncan Shearer and Lee Richardson from Blackburn and Mixu Paatelainen came from Dundee United. He also brought Paul Kane back into the team on a more regular basis, whereas he had been in and out previously. Jim Bett was also coming to the end of his time and he was being faded out. I still think he could have used me a bit more, though. I can understand wanting to play a different type of style but you also have to have another plan as well, a plan B if plan A doesn't work. I thought I could still do the business for Aberdeen, maybe not the way Willie wanted to, but he could have used me more than he did. I was only chosen to start two matches in my third season and came on as sub in two others, but he made the choice and you have to respect that choice, even if you don't like it.

There was one strange incident, though, that I still can't fathom out to this day. When I first arrived at Aberdeen from Groningen I had long hair and a moustache so I went to the hairdressers and said to them that I needed a haircut, and from then on I kept it shorter than I had it before. In my third season I had it a little bit longer, but not too long, and certainly nothing like it had been when I first came over. So there was this one time when I needed a haircut, so I made an appointment and got booked in for the following week. On the morning of the appointment we had a training session and beforehand I bumped into Willie in the boot room.

'Theo, you need a new haircut,' he told me.

When he said this I was a bit stunned. I thought it was quite a neat haircut I had, at least my wife didn't complain! Yes, it was a little bit longer than it had been previously but hardly anything to worry about. I didn't really know what to say. He was ignoring me as a player by then but was now talking to me about my grooming. Is he taking player management that far? In that case, let's talk about the moustache of Robert Connor, that was certainly an impressive growth! And what about Roy Aitken? He had a nice big haircut. Lee Richardson also had big hair, it was all over the place.

I said to him, 'I know it's a bit long so what would you like? Is there a Scottish style that I don't know about that I should have?'

By this time I was fed up. I knew I wouldn't have much time left at Aberdeen and I believed that Willie was acting not only for the best interests of the team but I believed that it was a personal thing now, too. As I said, I had quite coincidentally already made an appointment to have my hair cut that very day, so I contacted the hairdresser again. This was, of course, before the days of mobile phones, so I went to the club office and asked if I could make a phone call. I called the hairdresser and told them that because of certain circumstances I wouldn't be able to make it there this afternoon for my appointment and booked another one for three or four weeks later.

This incident was another little reason why I took what was happening personally. You can put me on the bench, you can decide that you don't like me as a person – sometimes that happens in football, you can't mix brilliantly with every single other person, that's impossible – but it should be about everyone as a football player and not as a character. Does this player do a good job on the field? Does he fit in with my way of playing? Those are the things you have to consider but I thought it was a bit disrespectful of him to order me to have a haircut!

I understand how difficult it is to be a coach or a manager. For me as a coach now, the case is that we can only put 11 players on the pitch and choose a few others as substitutes. I always feel sorry for the subs. It's a hard decision to leave people out and I make tough decisions for the boys. They all want to play but I have to say to them 'sorry, you're not in the team' and they have to show me in the training sessions that they're good enough or even better than the boys who are in the team. Sometimes I make mistakes and I have to put certain ones in again or take certain ones out, and maybe it means changing the system. It's all part of the game. The way I look at them is as football players and I don't make my decisions on the basis of someone's character or personality.

With Willie I felt that he looked at me as a football player but also had to say something about me as an adult, about my personality. I was 27 years of age, not a child anymore. Whether he was trying to be a big authority or not I don't know, but I don't like authority. This is only my opinion but if you want to win by being an authority, if you want to stamp your authority over everything, then you'll only end up in war. If I'm the authority and you all do as I say, then there's no discussion anymore. I would prefer to say that I want to discuss things, maybe even have an argument about them, where I give my opinion and you give your opinion. I want to discuss things as two people rather than as a coach with a player or a director with a coach. It should be equal and not based on the fact that I'm higher in rank than you are. That's maybe the difference with me and maybe why I seemed to clash with Willie, because if I do have a difference of opinion, I'll say so.

This was another difference between Dutch and Scottish football. Sometimes when we played in Holland the coach would say something to the captain to try to change the game and then the captain would go to the other players. He would tell them that the coach wants to change this and that and play this way or that way. We might think about it but then tell the captain that no, we're not going to do that, we're going to do this other particular thing instead. Then there were other times when things weren't going too well and the coach hasn't said anything when the players would just decide to change their style of play. Perhaps the coach had told us to sit back a little and soak up the pressure but, after 20 minutes or so, if things weren't going right, then we would change it. A player knows instinctively when a plan isn't working or if it isn't going to work – this player or that player is causing us trouble, this one is being given too much space, etc. – and we would take it upon ourselves to do something about it. That doesn't mean that we always had success, and we weren't doing that all the time, of course, because most of the time the coach would tell us what to do and we would do it, but sometimes we just had to change things out on the pitch. In Scotland there was a different kind of attitude among the players. What the boss says is what goes. If the boss says we go left, we go left. If the boss says we go right, we go right.

That was another thing, calling the coach 'Boss'. In Holland it wasn't like that, we would use their names. You would be the boss of your dog but with other people you use their names, so that was a bit of a surprise to me when I came over, as well. Of course I did it, though. If that was the way it was then that was the way it was. I called Alex Smith 'Boss', so nobody can say to me 'Theo, you didn't adjust', because I did. I called Jocky Scott 'Coach' and so on, never 'Alex' or 'Jocky' or 'Willie' or whatever.

There are different types of coaches but with each of them you need to have a good relationship. There are the more authoritarian coaches like Jose Mourinho, there are coaches like Erik ten Hag who are extremely organised, there are coaches like Carlo Ancelotti who is a gentleman and tactically very good, and there are different types of players, too. That's why it sometimes doesn't work with a particular coach and a squad of players, because their styles have to fit together. The thing is, though, no matter what sort of coach you have, the first thing you need to have is a good relationship between manager and players because without a good relationship you won't get success.

When I said previously that Willie is Mr Aberdeen, I didn't mean that in a sarcastic or disrespectful way. He really is Mr Aberdeen. Willie was a great football player, one of the best players Aberdeen ever had, maybe the best. His partnership with Alex McLeish was superb, absolutely world-class. You don't win league championships and trophies in Europe without having great players, especially in Willie's position in the heart of the defence. That position, that partnership between the two centre-backs, has to be rock solid because it's such a vital piece of the team. Also, as a manager he took Aberdeen to some cup finals in both the Scottish Cup and the Scottish League Cup, he took them back to business again. For that reason I can't say he was a terrible manager, he wasn't. We also finished runners-up in the league with him in charge.

Willie Miller is an Aberdeen legend and, when you look at everything he has achieved with the club, you can't argue with that. The only problem, I think, was merely that our styles and how we wanted to play football weren't the same.

Leaving Aberdeen

*If looks could kill, Willie would have
shot me down there and then.*

IN THE lead-up to the 1992/93 season, we went up to
Dingwall for a training camp and to play one or two friendly
matches. It was a good opportunity for the recent signings to
get to know their new team-mates. Duncan Shearer had been
brought in from Blackburn Rovers in England to be the new
centre-forward, with Hans Gillhaus on his way out of the club,
and Lee Richardson had also come up from Blackburn Rovers.
Shearer started every game alongside Mixu Paatelainen so it was
obvious that they were going to be the favoured attack. The trip
to the Highlands gave them a good chance to get to know one
another and see how each other played.

The friendlies all provided comfortable victories so were
good for the team's morale, but the main thing was to get fit
and ready for the start of the new season. Unfortunately, I had a
bit of an injury, only a minor one, as did Eoin Jess. Our physio,
David Wylie, told us to go out and do some cycling instead of
joining in with the training session as it would be a good thing
to help us get our fitness back without stretching us too far.

That sounded good to me. I'm from Holland and many people in Holland have a bicycle and do lots of cycling so, yeah, no problem by me. The only thing was that I didn't know my way around, it was the first time I had ever been there. Dingwall isn't that big but, even so, as soon as we left the camp I had absolutely no idea where we were going. So, we took the bikes out as the boys went to their training session, with Eoin leading the way.

It was all going fine, we were cycling along looking at the scenery and talking about the boys back at the base going through their training session. After a while at some point it started to get more and more difficult, the road becoming steeper and steeper. We were obviously cycling up a hill. As we all know, Holland isn't exactly renowned for its mountainous landscape but even I assumed they didn't call this part of Scotland the Highlands for nothing. Eoin, on the other hand, hadn't even realised that we were going upwards! So we kept going up. I don't know how long the road was but we were going for quite a way. Eventually we stopped and had to turn round again because we had been going for miles. I checked with Eoin that he was okay on his bike as I knew it wouldn't be a problem for me going down, I've been cycling all my life. 'No problem,' he said, so we started heading back down again.

'Okay, Eoin, just follow me,' I said, because when we got that far it really was quite steep, and on the upward journey had started to be quite hard work.

Heading down again wasn't so difficult, of course, and we got quite a speed up. A little way down I came to a corner so

119

I stopped and waited, expecting Eoin to be just behind me. I waited and waited and didn't see Eoin. I waited a while but there was no sign of him, so I started panicking a bit. I decided to turn round and climb up the hill again to see if I could find him. After a couple of hundred yards, round another corner, there he was sitting down on the grass. He was covered in mud and blood, having ridden straight into the bushes. Remember, this was in summer, it was beautiful weather, so we were just in shorts and T-shirts, so he had very little protection on his body.

'Eoin,' I said, 'I thought you could ride a bike.'

'Yes Theo, I know, but I missed the corner.'

'How come?'

'You went too fast so I couldn't turn in time and just decided to go straight ahead into the bush to stop myself.'

It wasn't really a bad injury that he had collected, he was just full of mud and dirt and it looked at first sight twice as bad as it actually was. He had a few cuts and scrapes on his arms and face, just the sort of thing you would expect if you ride straight into the bushes. So we sat down for a while, had a rest, had a laugh and then slowly, slowly went down the rest of the way. After an hour or so we arrived back at the hotel. As soon as we went in and the boys saw us, they started laughing, of course. They were sitting down in the hotel lobby, the training session had finished, they were all showered and clean and they were sitting down having a drink together. Then we walked in with Eoin looking the way he did and they all started laughing at us.

'Oh no, you've got to go and talk to Willie now,' they said, and then started to make a bit of a fool out of me, all in good humour, of course …

'No, don't speak to Willie, go to see Drew, he's your friend.'

'Drew will look after you.'

'Theo ten Caat and Drew Jarvie are best friends, you'll be fine.'

'It's not my fault Eoin Jess fell off his bicycle,' I said, 'he did it himself. He should have told me he can't ride a bike!'

I went to see David Wylie and told him a little accident had happened. I said to him that my injury is fine, I could probably train tomorrow, but Eoin has a bit of a problem with his ego now. I was just trying to make light of it because nothing serious had really happened, he only had a few scratches. We made a bit of a fool out of Eoin and he was laughing, we were all laughing. All except one. Willie Miller wasn't laughing. He was angry with me and said I should have taken care of Eoin.

'Why on Earth did you climb a mountain?' he asked me.

I thought this was rather unfair. I told him I didn't know. I had never been to this part of the world before. How was I to know that the road would suddenly become steep and high? When we were out we were just deciding to go left, go right, go left again, go straight on, we didn't really know where we were going. Suddenly we were on a kind of a hill but nothing I would exactly call a mountain. I asked Willie if it was my fault that Eoin had fallen off his bike. His answer was that I should have taken care of him and that I was responsible for the boy.

'Come on,' I said, 'you can't be serious. This must be a joke now. Nothing serious happened, we're all having a laugh about it.'

'Yeah, but he could have had a major incident or major accident, he could have broken his leg or his arm and then he's out for the rest of the season.'

I mean, yes, that sort of thing could have happened, but an accident could also happen in training. And what about me? I could have had an accident. I told him that I could understand that he was a little bit scared about what happened to Eoin Jess and, yes, it does look worse than it actually is, but don't make it into such a big thing. Everything is okay. He only has some scratches on his arm and a little bit of blood and mud. The boys are all laughing at us. They also warned me not to go straight to you, so I went to David Wylie first and he was fine. I don't know where Eoin is now, probably having a laugh and a pint with the lads, but now here I am sitting in here talking to you, trying to explain what happened and you make it bigger than it is, because nothing exciting happened. He let me go but he wasn't pleased. Me being out of favour at the time probably made it worse. If Eoin had been with Scott Booth or Duncan Shearer or any of Willie's favourites then it wouldn't have been such a problem. Maybe it was because I was Dutch and I know how to cycle, I don't know. The thing is, I can't ride somebody else's bike for them. In all honesty, I don't really know why he reacted in that way.

Anyway, these things happen. Now, whenever I think about Dingwall, I think about Eoin and his bicycle. Not even

Ross County, just Eoin sitting there on the grass up in the hills covered in mud.

There's another funny story, actually, involving a trip with some of the Aberdeen boys. This time it was during an international break. All the ones who were playing for their country had gone off. Mixu was with Finland, the Scottish internationals were all together wherever it was they were playing, Hans Gillhaus was with Holland, and we were only left with a few players really. Those of us remaining went to Majorca for a few days with the idea of doing some warm-weather training over there and having a bit of fun, too. We left on the Tuesday or Wednesday and came back on the Sunday, just a few days over there. When we were due to get back, our next game would be against Celtic, so they sent us away to Majorca before one of the biggest games of the season! Willie stayed in Aberdeen, with Roy and Drew coming over to Spain with us. The thing is, of course, going over to Magaluf is just party time. The whole place is basically set up for a good time. The only training sessions that we could manage while we were over there were two sessions of football tennis. And that was it. Before a game against Celtic. The rest of the time we were just hanging out and going out in the evenings.

This one particular night we all went out together but, because of the amount of people that were there and certain ones of us having their favourite bars or discos that they wanted to go to, throughout the course of the evening most of us got separated. I was with one particular player, and I won't mention his name, but we were sharing a room together on that trip, and at some point in the early hours of the morning I couldn't find him. It was time to get back to the hotel but he was nowhere to be seen. I decided to get a taxi back because if I looked for him I could have been out for the rest of the night until breakfast time and he had probably found some of the other players, anyway. He might even have gone back himself. I got back to the hotel and went up to our room but he wasn't there. I left the door on the latch so when he got back he could just come in without banging on the door and waking me up, and went to sleep. Next morning when I woke up, probably around 10.00 or so, I looked across to the other bed and there he was. He had obviously arrived back after I had gone to sleep as I hadn't heard anything. Let's be honest, I'd had my share as well.

'Where have you been?' I asked him when he woke up.

He said that sometime after we got separated out on the town, he got a taxi, like I did, to get back to the hotel. The problem was, though, that he couldn't remember what hotel we were staying in. Apparently, he had asked the taxi driver to just take him to the nearest hotel, where he got out, went into the reception, asked if he was staying there, and then when he was told he was in the wrong place, went to the next hotel and did the same thing. He was just going from hotel to hotel asking if they knew him. It took him more than an hour to find the correct one after visiting all the hotels in town. Not only that, but at about 5am, which was an hour on to the time at home, he decided to phone his wife to ask her if she knew where we were staying. So she got this phone call at 4am!

'Hello, love,' he had said to her, but then decided to start the conversation by saying, 'I'm not drunk.' I mean, you can imagine that she wasn't massively pleased to receive the phone call in the first place, but for her husband to start it with 'I'm not drunk' is just making it worse, isn't it?

'I've just called to ask if you know what hotel we're staying in,' he had said. 'I can't find it. I've got a taxi driver here on his meter and it's going to cost a fair bit.'

Fortunately his wife went easy on him, at least until he got back home, and she told him which hotel he wanted.

'You're a stupid guy,' I told him. 'You should know the name of the hotel you're staying in.'

'Yeah, but I was a bit drunk.'

'You should do what I do,' I said. 'Put a note in your pocket with the name of the hotel written on and then you wouldn't have had that problem.'

When we got back to Aberdeen on the Monday or Tuesday, we had a couple of days' training and then went to Celtic Park at the weekend. The game was actually quite a good one, quite even, and we went in at half-time behind by a single goal. When we all got into the dressing room, Willie Miller gave me a hairdryer. He was going into what apparently happened in Majorca – even though he wasn't there – and accused me of going out drinking and everything. Yes, okay, I'd had some, of course I had, but certainly not as much as most of the other boys. At that time, and things are a bit different now, but at that time the Brits abroad had a certain reputation but we Dutch didn't have that same sort of culture. Of course I was drinking, but the Dutch, especially Dutch sportsmen, were more moderate. I don't want this to sound like I'm such a goody-goody, but it's true. I liked a wine but I would also have water between drinks, which lessened the effect of the alcohol. Willie, though, was laying into me and telling me it was my fault that we were 1-0 down. All the other guys were looking at him, not really understanding why he was so irate at me.

'Hang on a minute, here,' I argued back at Willie. 'I'm the left-winger and I'm trying my best to attack. How is it my fault we're losing?'

I wasn't exactly happy with what he was saying so I took myself off to the toilet. Jim Bett followed me in and was urging me to calm down.

'You know what happens,' said Jim. 'If you play a nine out of ten, he's happy with you but if you play a six or a seven then you get a doing.'

I was substituted for Andy Roddie during the second half, not exactly unexpectedly, and at that point I really began to feel like I wasn't part of Willie's favourite squad. It just seemed that whatever I did wasn't going to be good enough.

Drew Jarvie had told me that I was the team's best football player but I wouldn't get much game time from Willie, and his words proved to be true. In that season I played in 15 of

Aberdeen's league matches, which was far less than most of the other midfield players. Paul Mason was playing virtually every match, Eoin Jess really made his mark that year, and Brian Grant, Lee Richardson, Roy Aitken, Paul Kane and Jim Bett were all in front of me in the number of appearances made. I'm not saying that these players were bad guys or anything like that, but it just proves how far down the order in Willie's mind I had fallen.

The following season was even worse. I only played four games for Aberdeen in that last season, all at Pittodrie. Three in the league against St Johnstone, Raith Rovers and Hearts and one in the League Cup, which was a 5-2 victory over Motherwell.

There was also a problem with the bonus payments. Even though I wasn't playing, I still felt that I was part of the team. We were all training together as we normally would, having our meals together, it's just that I wasn't being chosen to play in the games. Then the bonuses suddenly started to become a little erratic, so I went to see Willie in his office. To be honest, talking one to one with him was no problem whatsoever. In fact, we laughed a lot together. It just became a completely different situation when we were with the rest of the boys on the training pitch or in the dressing room, with him as coach and me as player. With regards to the bonuses, all of a sudden I was only receiving 50 per cent of what I had been previously. We spoke about it and he told me that, yes, I was still part of the team but, because I wasn't taking an active part in the matches, I should be happy that I received any money. I understood what he was saying. I didn't agree with it, but I understood it. Then, all of a sudden, the bonuses completely dried up, so I went to see him in his office again.

'There's something going wrong with the payments,' I told him. 'I'm not even getting 50 per cent anymore.'

'No, I stopped that one as well,' he said, 'because you're sitting in the stand and not participating with the team.'

'Hang on,' I argued back, 'I'm still training all week, so if I'm doing that I'm still influencing the team.'

But he wouldn't see my point of view. He said that that's the way it is, I was getting my wages that I was due for what I was doing during the week but that on Saturdays, when the games were on, there were different rules. Those that were in the stand and not part of the matchday squad, and I certainly wasn't the only one here, weren't getting the bonuses anymore.

'What about if I was injured?' I asked.

'Well, that would be different,' Willie answered. 'In that case you would still get your bonuses.'

'Well, in that case then,' I replied, 'I'm injured now.'

We made some light-heartedness out of it but I made my point to him. I've been with the team all week, I've been supporting them from the stand when, using Willie's own logic of not being part of the matchday squad and different rules being applied on the Saturdays, I could have been at home with my wife.

A young Theo in my under-12s team. I am the one in the front row holding the trophy.

A couple of years later in the Drenthe County under-15s team. That's me in the front row next to the goalkeeper.

A year later with the Drenthe under-16s. I am in the middle of the top row and Freddy is one from the right in the front.

With some of the lads at Hoogeveen.

Freddy and me in our stylish tracksuits around the time we were taken on by FC Twente.

Here we go!
My first season as a
professional footballer
with Twente in 1984.

At the Vincente Calderón Stadium before Groningen's big European night at
Atletico Madrid.

Celebrating with Rene Eijkelkamp after scoring against Madrid.

In the dressing room after the game with Martin Koopman, Henny Meijer and Eric Groeleken.

Alex Smith signed me for Aberdeen. He is one of the nicest people I have ever met in football.

Aberdeen, and especially Pittodrie, will always be home to me.

With Scott Booth after scoring my first goal Premier Division goal, the opener in a 4-1 win over St Mirren in October 1991.

Jostling with Rangers' Dale Gordon. To this day I still cannot abide Rangers

A photograph for a local paper when at Vitesse with a couple of ten Caat originals on the wall.

Signing my last professional contract at Twente

In action for Twente against Ajax.

Coaching in Canada. A wonderful experience that led to the formation of DutchCan Soccer.

Me today, keeping up with the news from Aberdeen, the club of my heart.

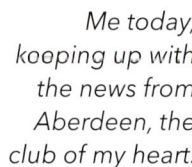

Our next match was an away game and we were in the hotel and I was sharing a room with Scott Thompson. On the morning of the match we didn't get our usual wake-up call at 8.00, so I overslept. Not by a huge amount, but about 30 minutes or so. Normally we would have received a knock on the door to make sure we were awake and up and about but this morning there wasn't one. So, I was lying awake in bed thinking to myself, *I know I'm not playing but have they just forgotten about me now!?* So I just stayed in bed, lying there waiting to see if the knock would come. By 9.00 still nothing and still Scott was asleep in the other bed. At 10.00, David Wylie, our physio, eventually knocked on the door and came in.

'Oh,' I said, 'is it 8.00? Can we wake up for breakfast?'

The look on his face! 'Come on Theo, get up, it's 10.00, we have to leave now!'

Scott eventually woke up due to all the kerfuffle and he started panicking.

'Come on, get a move on,' David was urging us, 'everyone else is in the bus waiting for you guys.'

'Well then, why did you not knock earlier?' I asked. 'You knew we were late, why have you only just come up?'

By the time I had asked him this, Scott had jumped out of bed and was in his football kit in about 30 seconds flat. I took a little bit more time getting ready, so was the last person to get on the bus. All the boys were laughing at me and shouting at me, all in good humour, but, if looks could kill, Willie would have shot me down there and then. This is understandable,

I suppose, because for the lads it was all a bit of a laugh but for management it's a bit more serious. But then Roy Aitken decided that he would give me a bit of a doing. Willie stayed calm as a normal manager would. Okay, he gave me a bit of a look, but he stayed calm, not wanting to waste any energy or create a bad vibe before a match with a player that he wasn't going to use anyway, but Roy went for me, telling me how bad my behaviour was and that I was this and I was that.

'Well, Celtic man,' I said to him, 'you just sit down there. You're an assistant manager. If there's a problem, the manager will do the talking.'

Whether he thought he was impressing the team by playing manager, I don't know, but I was having none of it. 'Roy, you're a player today,' I said, 'and I'm not going to accept those words because today you're a colleague of mine. After the whistle you can act like an assistant manager if you wish to and I'll listen to you. Now, though, you're in the bus and you're a player today, so you're a footballer just as I'm a footballer and all these other guys are footballers. If any of the others decided they wanted to give me a doing I would say to them exactly as I've said to you. Just concentrate on the game and don't get involved with me because I'm fed up now because nobody knocked on the door to get us up. I'm late and it isn't only my fault, there has been fault with the organisation.'

All the boys were laughing, ducking down a bit and turning around pretending they were looking out of the window so as not to make it so obvious. I sat down, the bus drove off, we had the game, I watched from the stand, we all came back again, and that was it, nothing. Not a single word was said about it. That was the last time I went to an away game with the first team. I knew that my team-mates shouldn't really have seen this, so I went to Willie during the week and said to him that the situation was no good for me and it wasn't respectful for him or for Roy and Drew and certainly not respectful for the other players. I told him that I knew there was no chance of him picking me again and that I had made the decision not to join the first team anymore. I also told him that I did want to carry on playing football for Aberdeen Football Club and asked to be put in with the second team.

To be honest, I had a really good time playing with the reserves. Neil Cooper was the manager then, with Teddy Scott helping him. I really enjoyed helping to bring the younger boys on, playing and winning games with them. There were some really great lads there, people like Stephen Glass, Hugh Robertson, Andy Roddie sometimes, although he was often with the first team as well. Football-wise I had fun. It was a little bit frustrating, of course, because, without trying to blow my own trumpet, I knew I was among the better football players at the club, but that's the way it goes sometimes. I really did enjoy those times with the second team.

To be fair to Aberdeen, they did try to get me to move away so I could start playing first-team football again elsewhere, but they were asking for too much money as a transfer fee. Swindon Town were interested, which would have been a brilliant move for me at the time because they were in the English Premier League. They had gained promotion the previous year under the management of Glenn Hoddle, who then left to go to Chelsea, and were now being managed by John Gorman, who once again joined up with Hoddle as an assistant when he became the England manager a couple of years later. Another couple of teams in England were also interested in me as well as Vitesse and Groningen back in Holland, but a transfer never came about so I stayed until the end of the season.

During that summer I was sort of just waiting to hear where I would be playing next but, when it came to reporting back for pre-season training, I was still an Aberdeen player. A move finally came about right at the end of the pre-season and I returned to Holland with Vitesse.

As I've said, Aberdeen was a completely different style of football to what I was used to in Holland, and living there was a completely different style of life, but I loved it. I loved living in Aberdeen. I've taken youth teams that I've coached over to Scotland to play tournaments and to train there, and I always loved meeting up with Chic McLelland, who was working on the youth development side at Aberdeen. I was sad when I heard that he had passed away a few years ago. He was always so enthusiastic about what he was doing and it was always lovely to meet up with him. I'm sure he's very much missed around the club.

I do like returning to Aberdeen to visit, I love the place. I love Pittodrie. I know the club are looking to move on to a new stadium somewhere and I understand why, with all the finances involved and money and investors, but I do think it's a shame. I love the outside of the stadium with Aberdeen Football Club written in the bricks in the wall, I think it's fantastic. It gives a real sense of history. It's almost like a museum. You can't throw that away. Just ask me to help. I'll come along with my son, who is an architect.

The fans of the club are brilliant, too, and they're not just all situated within the city of Aberdeen. In my first year at the club I was asked to go up to Orkney. I have to admit, and I apologise to the people of Orkney, but I had never heard of it. Alex Smith told me there were a lot of supporters up there and it would be nice to go up and see them. I said okay and asked how long it would take to drive there, but he told me, no, you have to go up in a plane, it's in the islands above the mainland. So we went up there, we landed in a little airport in Kirkwall, and it was nice. I also had to do a speech, even though I didn't know this until we actually got there. I hadn't long been in the country, it would be my first-ever speech in the local language and I was extremely nervous. Had I known before I actually got there, I would have prepared something, but now I just had to improvise, but it was fine. It was actually a good piece of learning for me. We had some really good fun with the supporters during my time at Aberdeen and that was really nice. The club has a good relationship with their fan base, an unusually good relationship, and I think that's a really good and important thing.

* * *

Talking with Theo about leaving Aberdeen, the conversation suddenly took a reflective turn. The mood changed and he became more contemplative, philosophical even. He began to take a bit more time in answering and making sure he chose exactly the right words to use. He started to focus on the mid-distance as if actually replaying in his mind thoughts and questions he may have had at the time that he has since boxed away. It was actually quite moving. I feel at this point it serves the narrative better to reproduce it as the conversation it was. I started by asking why he thought it might have ended the way it did under Willie Miller …

TtC: As a manager you have to understand that no matter how good you are as a player, some players are never going to be as good as you were. You have to understand their weaknesses and try to find out why they made the mistakes they did. That's what I try to do with my team, FC Emmen under-21s. Sometimes in training the midfielders and the wide players will put in terrible crosses and I say to them, 'Give me the ball and I'll show you,' and I put in good crosses. I don't have to think about giving a good ball because I don't feel the pressure, but it's them who feel the pressure. They're thinking it has to be a good ball, even in a training session. I tell them, 'That's why you give a bad ball, because you're thinking. Don't think, just play it into the box.' Throughout my career I've given so many crosses that what I'm doing is no longer in my head, it's all natural, it's a reflex. When you're a good player, what you have to understand is that when you become a manager what's normal for you may not be normal for somebody else because they're not as good as you were. They make mistakes you would never make. Then, being the coach, you have to solve the problem. Marco van Basten didn't make it as a coach. Why? Because he couldn't understand why people made the mistakes that they did, so was unable to solve the problem. Willie Miller was so good as a football player but was he good as a coach? Did he win trophies? How long was he the manager?

NB: He was there for three years, pretty much three years to the day, I think. February 1992 to February 1995.

TtC: I think that maybe he'd had enough after the three years because the players maybe couldn't understand what he wanted and he got a little bit frustrated. I can understand this looking at him as a player. Was Alex Ferguson a good player?

NB: He played at the top level. He was a centre-forward, he played for Rangers. Played a few times for Scotland as well.

TtC: He did understand why players made mistakes and would talk about it. He also had the philosophy that the most important thing was what was good for the team, not the individual. That's the reason that he occasionally let top players go from Manchester United, players that carried on having a good career elsewhere.

NB: He did that all through his time at United, didn't he? The one who became the big star and maybe started to hog the headlines, perhaps to the detriment of some others maybe, he would put in their place. Some of them he let leave the club. David Beckham is the obvious example, but there were also players like Paul Ince, Jaap Stam …

TtC: That's how it goes. Willie was a brilliant player and had so much success, so much success. He could keep Ibrox quiet and Celtic Park quiet and that has to have something to do with your personality. Nobody can silence Ibrox, but Willie Miller could. When you're that good you have to make sure that reality stays with you.

NB: But he did have a measure of success. In 1992/93 Aberdeen were runners-up in both the Scottish Cup and the League Cup.

TtC: Yes, he did. I wish I could have a word with Willie. It would be interesting if we could talk now.

NB: I wonder what reasons he would give?

TtC: Yes. I'm interested in his point of view about me as a person and a football player, I'm really interested. What happened at the end of my Aberdeen time? I mean, I was almost an international in Holland when I left Groningen and I was doing pretty good with Alex Smith, but then Willie comes and it all breaks down. I'm not completely blaming Willie, I have to blame myself as well. Sometimes lives take strange roads. I hope one day I get a chance to sit down with Willie and talk with him about how he looks at me. I know I can be a pain in the neck sometimes, I know that, but I think I'm a nice guy. I like trying to help people. The problem is that I can't handle it when I think there has been an injustice, and losing my place in the team when I did, I thought was an injustice. Now that I'm a coach I know that that can sometimes be annoying for coaches. I do respect those guys now, but I'm still trying to understand their actions. I was having a hard time, mentally as well. It wasn't easy in that last year. I knew I was going to go back to Holland, but what would the future bring? I had a wife and a young child and we were living somewhere I liked, where people were nice. Ideally, I would have played there for six, seven, eight years, but then it all broke down.

NB: Would you have considered moving to another Scottish club rather than go back to Holland?

TtC: I don't know, I don't know. Maybe I would have. Peter van de Ven went to Hearts but I don't think I should have gone to Hearts. I don't know. Would I go to ... no. Old Firm? No. Not after being an Aberdeen player, I could never go to Celtic or Rangers. Dundee United? No. Which team would have suited me? Probably Hibs the most. No, I should have stayed with Aberdeen.

NB: It's playing time though, isn't it? That's what every footballer wants.

TtC: That's the thing. They tried to sell me during the third year but I said, 'No, no, no, I'm staying here for three years. I'm not leaving half a year before the end of my contract and going to every team you find. If there's no team I want coming in for me before the end of the season I'll go back to Holland.' I also thought that if it didn't work out then I might quit football. I was sick and tired of what was happening. I really felt at home there, despite the problems. Teddy Scott helped me a lot, Neil Cooper as well, Andy Roddie, Scott Thompson, all those guys. We had lots of laughs and made the best out of it. When he was having his team talk, Neil Cooper would always say, 'You know?' After every sentence he said, 'You know?' Apart from not being in the first team, it was a brilliant time. We always went to McDonald's after the game. He used to pick me up by the roundabout at the Bridge of Dee. I would park my car there, the bus would come and pick us up, we would go to the game and McDonald's afterwards. The last year was a lot of fun with the boys in the reserve team.

At this last part, Theo's eyes genuinely lit up and the smile returned to his face. I was convinced that he really did enjoy his time at Aberdeen and wasn't just saying so for the sake of this book. He had made it clear throughout that, despite things not always going the way he would have liked on the pitch, Aberdeen Football Club really was a special place to be.

I hope Theo does get the chance to sit down with Willie one day, and I don't see why they shouldn't. They're two former Aberdeen players who were both doing what they thought was right for the club. Okay, their philosophies may have been a little different, but they're still in the ex-Dons club together. The respect that Theo has for Willie as a player is blatantly obvious and he acknowledges his place in the club's history. At the time of writing it has been about 30 years since Theo left Aberdeen. There's surely a table in the corner of a little pub somewhere with a couple of whiskies on it just waiting for the two of them to sit down …

Aberdeen Team-mates

FROM OUR conversations, it's clear that, despite the fact that his career at Aberdeen didn't necessarily go as might have at first been anticipated, Theo really did enjoy his time in Scotland. Even when talking about his exit from the club, he still has a glint in his eye at the thought of some of the characters he came across at Pittodrie. I got the feeling that if he had somehow managed to arrive there at a different time with different circumstances and was told he could stay for as long as he wanted, he would still be there now. I took some time to just throw a few names at him to see what his first reactions would be. At the mention of some of these names a big smile came across Theo's face …

Teddy Scott

The first time I met Teddy Scott was in the kit room. I always liked to get to training early to give myself plenty of time to get ready, especially when I first arrived at Aberdeen. I was living in a hotel at the time, which I didn't really like much because, no matter how nice or comfortable the hotel is, it isn't your own house with all of your things around. I always came to the club to have my breakfast, then I would go and see Teddy. We would have nice talks and he would help me a lot. In some ways he was more of a coach for me than the official coaches. We had two co-managers, Alex Smith and Jocky Scott, and then we also had Drew Jarvie with whom I had a good understanding, and then we had Teddy. He was always in the kit room and we would have a coffee and talk many times.

I remember when I first joined the club, getting a big surprise in the shower room. We had a lot of showers and we also had a big bath. In Holland it goes that you always have a shower after a training session and then you jump into the bath, so I assumed it would be the same here. At Aberdeen it was completely different.

The players first of all jumped into the bath, washed themselves and shaved themselves, and the first time I was sitting there thinking, *What's happening here?* I got everybody else's dirty stuff – bits off mud, shampoo, beard shavings – floating towards me. I was sitting with all of this stuff coming towards me, pushing the water back, trying to get it all away from me. Why did I want everybody else's dirt coming to me when I'm trying to get myself clean?

I said to Teddy, 'What's this? We've got a shower where they can shave.'

He said, 'Theo, this is how we do it.'

I wasn't convinced. 'Do you really think, sitting in among the mess of 20 other people, that I'm going to take a bath after a training session?'

Teddy just looked at me and smiled. He knew. Sure enough, I was soon in the bath with the rest of them, shaving myself and washing my hair and thinking nothing of it.

Only a small thing, perhaps, but that's what Teddy did. He helped me in all sorts of ways. He taught me to go with the flow, relax, no stress, and his door was always open.

I spent a lot of hours with Teddy and he explained to me how the Scottish League worked. A nice place for a football player to go to when he just needs a little bit of peace and quiet is the kit room. Often I went in and sat down and just looked around all the boots. They were all in the same place, everybody had their own space where they sat. Sometimes I would sit there for 30 minutes with Teddy working there. Even if he wasn't there it was a nice place to just go and sit and relax. We would just talk as he went about his business, analysing the games or the training sessions, what I did good or what I did bad. We would also talk about relationships between everybody at Aberdeen. I'm the type of guy who analyses a lot, not only on the playing side in games and training sessions but also with relationships. Not just relationships with my team-mates, but with everyone around the club, even the ones in the kitchens. They're important people too, they do a lot of work for you, and I never want to forget that. Sometimes I took my time just to sit down for half an hour in the kit room and just think about everybody who is around. Then you find that your mind starts flowing. You start thinking about the history of the club.

In Teddy's room all the shirts were hanging there, and that, for me, was one of the special places. It just had a certain atmosphere. Shirts of all the former players, the really important players who had helped in the history of Aberdeen to make the club what it is, were hanging there. There were old pictures of former players, too, and I really liked the history of the club. I always like to go into Pittodrie through the front door. It's a big oak door, and when you open it and go through – bang! – you see Aberdeen FC on the floor, you see the big European trophy – I can always picture this in my mind. Aberdeen love their history and they respect their history and those sorts of things made a big impression on me. I love the feeling when you enter a room and you can just smell and taste what's gone before, all the big players that have been there before you. For me, that's one of the best things, it's one of the big reasons I played football. That's what I'm like as a person. I'm really influenced by history and emotions.

We talked a lot, especially in the early days, about the differences between Scotland and Holland. We discussed how the football was different. We used to use his blackboard to draw tactical plays and discuss which ones might work and which ones might not. I would show him what was popular in Holland and he would draw up what was more popular in Scotland. We talked a lot about tactics.

Teddy was a father figure to me, especially in that first year. He knew it was a difficult transition for me from Dutch football to Scottish football so he was always there for me to talk to. Even if he wasn't in his room when I went to see him I would stay in there for a bit of reflection on things that were happening and how I was. When you do that it's really interesting the kind of ideas that come into your head. What am I doing wrong? When things don't turn out so good is it really my fault? Teddy was like a guide for me. He took really good care of me when I was struggling under Willie Miller and Roy Aitken. There was a point where they took away my match bonuses even though I was still a member of the first-team squad. At some point towards the end of my second year I didn't get any bonuses anymore even though I always travelled with the first team. I had a wee word with Willie about it and even suggested that I play in the reserve team because at least then I would stay match fit. I was fit enough for the training sessions but I needed to play games. I spoke a lot with Teddy about this situation. He didn't say an awful lot but I understand why, I knew he couldn't say too much and be seen to be criticising the manager of the club, but from the human aspect he really understood my frustration at that time.

If you look at Teddy Scott as a person you see how important he was for Aberdeen. He worked there for 50 years. He was a player, a coach and also the kit man. He is a very special person in the history of the club. It was Teddy who made Willie Miller the player he became. When Willie was playing in the reserves he was playing as a forward and Teddy told him he had to become a central defender. That shows what a brilliant eye he had for a player.

Apparently, for one European match in the early days of Alex Ferguson, Teddy had brought the wrong shirts for the players to wear and Ferguson got so mad that he threatened to sack him. It was only the players intervening and getting across to Ferguson how important Teddy was to the club that saved him. It's a good job they did because Aberdeen would have been a poorer place without Teddy Scott involved.

Teddy is deservedly in the Aberdeen Hall of Fame. He was one of my favourite men.

Alex McLeish

Alex McLeish as a player was, at that time, as important as Willie Miller had been in the 80s. He was the main man. I learned a lot from him. I still remember one incident with him. In Holland, most of the players would use metal studs in their boots, but in Scotland they didn't. They just had normal rubber moulded studs. We had one particular training session where we came in and had breakfast and then went out on to the pitch. Actually, in that matter, Scottish football was far ahead of Dutch. We always had breakfast together before the training session, and lunch together afterwards, but we never had that in Holland. We had breakfast at home, had our training and then also lunch on our own. Anyway, this one day I had my metal studs in and I kicked Alex McLeish really hard.

'Theo, what kind of shoes are you wearing?' he asked me.

I looked at the sky and said, 'Alex, it's raining, and in Holland if it's raining we have our studs in, our real studs.'

'Well,' he said, 'you're not in Holland now, lad, you're in Scotland. If you train with those boots ever again, I'm going to give you a really hard time. I'll be chasing you for the whole training session and I don't think you'll make it back to the dressing room.'

It was more of a joke than a threat, I hope, but he isn't the sort of person that you want to upset.

Actually, that was another thing that surprised me about Scottish football. In Holland nearly every team has their own training ground, but when I went to Scotland we had to go to the park – Seaton Park or sometimes Hazlehead Park. The young boys got there early and had to make up the goals. They left on the buses earlier, they left at 9.30, we started training at 10.00. We were running through the trees in the park, which, actually, was a nice surprise for me because I like nature.

One thing that happened at Setaon Park was we had the Seaton Park run. This was apparently a traditional thing for the Aberdeen players. The Seaton Park run was about five kilometres, mostly uphill, and then another kilometre down again, this part being very short and steep. Stuart Kennedy had held the club record for years but, during the time when Willie Miller and Roy Aitken were in charge of the team, I beat the time, but Willie was having none of it.

'I'm not counting it,' he decided. 'Theo has been out for some weeks injured so has been running all the time to get his fitness back. He has an unfair advantage so Kennedy still has the record.'

It didn't really bother me that much, I just laughed at them.

We always had a training session on the Friday before a match and we used to play a game where you're standing two on two and we had to run left to right. We had different-coloured cones – blue, red, yellow, green – and we had to go here and there, to this one and that one. We had heats and the losers were out and the winners went on until there was a final. If you won then all well and good, but if you were the runner-up you were 'the donkey'. Guess who was always the donkey …? I was always going wrong, so every Monday morning had to wear the yellow jersey of shame.

Overall, the training sessions were quite hard. There was a lot of running and it was really physical. The football games during the sessions weren't really that physical, we just played normal games. There wasn't really a lot of tactics in them. Let's say, for example, we were due to play Rangers. We never heard such things as: 'What are their strengths? Where can we hurt them?' Those kinds of things just weren't discussed. In Holland it was always: 'How should we play against this opponent? What organisation? Shall we play 4-3-3 or 4-4-2? Shall we use a diamond or shall we play flat?' All these kinds of things we used to talk about during the week but that didn't seem to happen so much in Scotland.

Anyway, Alex McLeish was the one that we all looked up to. He was just a brilliant defender. When he was out of the team because of injury it was a big reason why we didn't get the results we should have, which eventually led to Alex Smith losing his job. We really missed him when he wasn't playing. In tight games somebody would make one mistake and it would be a goal. I'm sure that wouldn't have happened had Alex been playing.

I always had respect for Alex and listened to what he said to me about the game. He had played hundreds of times, won everything in the Scottish game, and I was just a lad in my mid-20s. I had watched him play against Real Madrid and Bayern Munich, winning the European Cup Winners' Cup, and it was a pleasure to play in the same team as him.

Duncan Shearer

Duncan Shearer was a brilliant guy, very funny. He was also superb in front of goal. I always used to say that if we had the ball in our half and Duncan was calling for it on the halfway line, don't give it to him. If you did, the ball would just bounce ten yards off him and it would be gone. If you played the same ball to him near the penalty box, though, that would be a completely different story. In that situation the ball would be like glue on his feet. It was amazing how different the two circumstances could be. With the ball in the box he was lethal, but with the ball in midfield he would lose it. He was a brilliant striker, so important for Aberdeen at that time. He scored a lot of goals. Whoever he played with, be it Eoin Jess or Scott Booth or Mixu Paatelainen, they did really well and he just seemed to gel with them.

Peter van de Ven

One day Peter told me he had a problem with his car and asked if he could come into training with me the next day.

We didn't live far away from each other so I said yes, of course I could give him a lift in. The next morning, though, I completely forgot about it and drove to the club as I normally would. After I had gone, Peter came to my house and knocked on my door and my wife answered and told him that I had already left.

'What do you mean he has already left?' he asked.

'Well, he has already left.' What else could she say?

The problem was I only realised I was supposed to collect Peter when I arrived at Pittodrie. Had I remembered any earlier I could have turned round and gone to get him, but now it was too late. I remember sitting in my car feeling terrible. So I went into training telling myself that people make mistakes, people forget things, basically trying to comfort myself. Eventually Peter arrived and he didn't say anything. Not a word. If I had been in that situation, I would have said to Peter, 'Peter, if you didn't want to take me with you, you could have just told me,' and made a bit of a joke about it. But he was really quite angry at me and he didn't talk to me for a couple of days. After a while I thought I had better go and talk to him before the situation got completely out of hand and it became a problem.

'Alright, Peter, I made a mistake, I'm sorry,' I said, 'but how many mistakes do you make in a game?'

I didn't say it in an accusing or confrontational way, I was just trying to be funny.

'I make lots of mistakes in a game and now I've made a mistake in the car when I forgot that I was supposed to take you with me. Are you still angry with me? If you are, just say it. Tell me so and then we can move on.'

'It's okay Theo, I'm not angry with you,' he said. 'Everything is clear now.'

Now that we'd had the conversation we could move on but it took almost a week. I would have settled it within one hour, made a joke out of it. I would have gone into the dressing room and in front of everybody said, 'If you don't want to take me in your car, and I can understand that because you've got a smashing car and you don't want me to dirty your seats, hello, but just tell me and I'll take a bus or cycle.'

But that's Peter. He can't help it, he's from Limburg in the southern part of Holland. He's not like us northerners. They've got no sense of humour there apart from in the annual carnival that they hold!

I say this tongue in cheek, of course …

Hans Gillhaus

Hans is one of the best players I've played with. He was tremendous. What he did at Aberdeen was amazing. I was sad when he left because not only was he a great player but I socialised a lot with him. After games I would always go to his house and we would talk about the game over a coffee and a pizza. After an away game we always used to go to the McDonald's in Union Street and sit down for an hour and talk about things. If we won the game, that was. If we lost we would order the McDonald's, take it out and go and eat it at

Hans's house. We had some really nice times together, times where we could sit and talk about things away from the club, away from that pressurised environment, so we were free to say what we wanted to say and what we meant. It was a shame when he left and I missed him, but that's football. People move on.

Drew Jarvie

Drew is just a nice guy. He's one of the only coaches that I can remember not having arguments with, him and Alex Smith and Teddy Scott, of course. When I say arguments, I don't mean shouting at each other or anything like that, I mean about the way to play football. The problem with me is that I'm open, whereas most footballers are closed, they're afraid of saying something that others might not like. I don't like playing politics, that's not how I operate. I tried to, I tried really hard, but I just can't. If a coach tells me something then I give him a straight answer, how I feel about it. If what I say is contrary to what he thinks, then okay, that's the way it is. It isn't only with Willie Miller that I had these sorts of discussions, these fights, it's almost every coach. I want to win and I have a vision of how I want to play football. With Drew, though, I don't think I ever had one of these disagreements.

During his career he was also a great football player, a great striker. He had a prolific partnership with Joe Harper, another Aberdeen legend. Drew played almost 400 games and scored well over 100 goals for the club.

The only thing that wasn't good about Drew was his hair! He was always pushing it back over his head with his hand because it kept falling off like Bobby Charlton's used to. If you live in Scotland near to the sea with the wind blowing you spend an awful lot of time brushing your hair back into place! If I had to keep doing that I would have gone to the barber and said, 'Come on, cut it off, let me go bald.'

I joke, of course, because I had a really good relationship with Drew Jarvie. As people we just understood each other as characters and as personalities. I only have good memories about him. He's a gentleman, he's modest, he's honest, a real Aberdeen man. He gave me a lot of advice and I'll never forget that.

Eoin Jess

When I came over to Scotland, Eoin was just a youngster and hadn't been in the first team squad for that long. He and Scott Booth were coming up at the same time. Because they were youngsters, though, they had to make sure that the kit and the balls and everything were there when we started our training session. In fact, that's what I've done when I'm training my boys in Holland. I tell them that the young boys have to make sure everything is alright. They ask me, 'Why the young boys?' and I say to them, 'Let me tell you a story,' and I tell them that when I was at Aberdeen we had two young boys called Eoin Jess and Scott Booth, and I tell them to go and look them up on the internet. I tell them that they were in the first team and were on their way to becoming internationals but still they had to look after the rest of us and make sure everything was ready for training.

Eoin is a really nice guy. He's polite and humble. I sometimes think that he was a bit too humble, and with a bit more selfishness or self-assuredness he could have raised his game to an even higher level. Scott, on the other hand, was a lot more self-confident. He was always there and he always had something to say, whereas Eoin was happy to stay a bit more in the background. If you could have moulded the two together, if Eoin Jess had the bravado of Scott Booth then, in my opinion, he could have become an international superstar. He was that talented.

I could see a lot of similarities between Eoin and me personality-wise. I liked trying to help others and making sure they were okay, and was sometimes perhaps a little too focused on that rather than being a little bit more selfish and concentrating on just myself. Eoin was the same. Now I'm a bit older and a coach rather than a player, looking back I do wish Eoin had been a little bit more selfish. Not only on the pitch but off it as well. I would have loved to have seen him being a bit more protective of himself and his views, being a bit more forthright, showing how he feels and putting forward his arguments more. He could have looked in a mirror and said, 'I'm Eoin Jess and I'm the best footballer in Scotland,' but he would look in the mirror and say, 'I'm Eoin Jess and I'm doing pretty good at Aberdeen.' The attitude you take on can raise you to another level above the rest or can help you to catch up with the rest. Either that or it can stop you taking that last step and allow others to catch up with you.

Having said that, Eoin still had a great career. He played and scored goals for his country and was voted into Aberdeen's greatest-ever team by the supporters. I'm pleased for him, he deserves those honours.

Paul Mason

Paul is a nice guy, he's a brilliant guy. He played for Groningen as well, but we just missed each other. He played there from 1984 to 1988 when he joined Aberdeen, and my period at the club began in 1988. Paul was a good player. I was playing out on the left with Grantie and Jim Bett in the middle, and Paul played on the right. At Groningen he was playing as a full-back but was always a midfielder in Scotland. He was good when running with the ball, he was a good crosser, he was strong, pretty much all you want from a midfielder.

Paul was one of my room-mates during my time at the club, and if I don't like a person then I'm not going to let them sleep in my room. I had no problem with Paul – he was and still is an English gentleman.

Vitesse Arnhem

*He picked the ball up and drop-kicked it 100
yards away. 'This is my pass to you, Theo,' he
said. 'Go and collect the ball and then you cannot
complain anymore.'*

MY MOVE to Vitesse came about because of an injury to one
of their players. The pre-season was virtually over so I hadn't
really had much time to get used to being at the club and with
my new team-mates before the season began.

Hans Gillhaus had also made the move to Vitesse from
Aberdeen the previous season and it was expected that he was
going to move on again, this time to Japan. Such was the deal
between Aberdeen and Vitesse that if Hans did move on in a
certain amount of time then Aberdeen also would receive some
money as part of that transfer as well. Hans did eventually move
to Japan, but not straight away, and we had six months playing
together again. It wasn't until the winter of 1994 that he joined
Gamba Osaka in the J-League. The Japanese league had only
been professional for a couple of years by then – before that it
was run on an amateur basis – and they were trying to import
some good players from Europe and South America to give it a

boost and to bring some names in to help it get off the ground. The Brazilians were particularly popular with people of the calibre of Careca, Dunga and Leonardo, all world-class players in their prime.

Ton van Dalen, my agent, had called me to say that Vitesse had come in and wanted to sign me. Karel Aalbers was the chairman then and he did a really good job at the club. He had taken over in 1984 when the club was in the second division and his vision was to put Vitesse among the top teams in Europe. Now here we were ten years later and they were in the top league, with a new stadium with more than double the capacity of the previous one, and they had also gained some European experience as well. There were some very good players at the club too, as well as Hans Gillhaus. A young Roy Makaay was there, just beginning to make his way in the game. He went on to have such a great career in Spain with Deportivo La Coruña and in Germany with Bayern Munich, as well as playing for the Dutch national team. Phillip Cocu was also there before he became a star for PSV and Barcelona. He went on to win 100 international caps. Glenn Helder and Raimond van der Gouw as well, before they went to Arsenal and Manchester United, respectively. Ante Mise was there. He was a Croatian international, and so was Dejan Čurović of Serbia, so we had a good team.

My first day at Vitesse was a Friday and a strange thing happened when I got back home that evening. I was sitting there with my wife and we were chatting, and I just had the feeling that perhaps I hadn't made the right decision. I just felt that maybe I had been pushed in that direction. Of course, I knew about Vitesse as a club, the players that were there and the way they liked to play, but there was just this feeling that it wasn't necessarily the right club for me at that time.

Herbert Neumann was the coach. He had been a popular midfield player with FC Köln in his day and had even represented the German national team. He was also a bit of a philosopher. I had many talks with him in his office and he was such an interesting guy. He would talk about life issues and everything. When we spoke about football, though, it was obvious that he had his favourites and I got the impression that when I joined the club they didn't really involve him in the transfer and that maybe he might not even have known about what was happening until I had signed. I think, actually, that it was the board who bought me and they had said to him, 'Here you are, we've got you another player.' The thing is, they had an injury to one of their players and I think I was signed to replace him, even though the manager didn't actually ask for a replacement! Neumann's assistant was Jan Jongbloed, who had been the Dutch goalkeeper in the 1974 World Cup. Whether he knew I was being signed either, I don't know, but here I was.

Our first friendly game was against an amateur team, and on the morning of the game we had a light training session followed by lunch together. We had the afternoon to ourselves before the evening kick-off, so one of the players asked if I wanted to go into the city for a poker game. So I went along with a couple of the guys to this particular pub in the city, and on the way there they warned me that sometimes they played for big money so it might be best that I just watched for a while and if I decided I was up to it, join in then. When the game started there were five of us round the table.

'If you want to join, you have to put down 25 guilders first,' I was told, 'and you can go up as high as 500.'

'Hang on a minute,' I said, 'no way, boys. I'm not laying down that much. I'm out of the game. I'll just watch you play.'

The game started and I just sat there watching, and it started getting quite intense. At times there were more than 4,000 guilders on the table. I couldn't believe what I was seeing. These were team-mates gambling big-time against each other. I later found out that some players were in debt for more than 30,000 guilders! I know footballers had a bit of a reputation in those days for their card schools, but not to this degree, surely? How could you have a good relationship with a guy in those circumstances? You train together and play together and you're supposed to work up good relationships on the pitch, but how can you when you owe them 30,000 guilders? Plus, there are family responsibilities to think about, too. I made sure I stayed away from that scene. How could I possibly go home to my wife and tell her I had lost that amount of money, even just a couple of hundred? That would mean no meals for us for a while! That was my first encounter with Vitesse.

Our first league game provided us with a hard start to the season against PSV and they beat us 4-2. They were a quality team. They had Ronaldo up front, Stanley Menzo in goal, Jan Wouters was their captain, the Belgian Luc Nilis was their playmaker, Gheorghe Popescu, Boudewijn Zenden, a really good line-up. A really difficult start for us.

I played a few games at the start of the season but my player-manager relationship with Herbert Neumann wasn't the greatest, probably because, as I've already said, I wasn't really his player. The board had signed me pretty much behind his back. Whether Jongbloed knew of the signing, I don't know but, because Neumann had his favoured picks, I was in and out of the team. I even joked that I would be up against the reserve goalkeeper for a place in the starting line-up and that he was a good shout to play on the left wing. After a couple of months I was pretty sure that my initial reaction, when I told my wife that it might have been a mistake to sign, was the right one. The newspapers got hold of the fact and a couple of teams were interested in taking me on during the season, but the transfer fee that was put on my head would have been too expensive for them.

I played 14 games for Vitesse that season – it wasn't really a successful marriage. A couple of players left throughout the course of the season, as well. Hans Gillhaus finally made his move to Japan and Glenn Helder was signed by Arsenal. He was George Graham's last signing as Arsenal manager and, strangely, never played a game for him. Graham was sacked by the club after a Premier League enquiry found that he had accepted illegal payments from an agent during a couple of transfer dealings. Graham was relieved of his position on the morning of Helder's debut.

Helder was something else. First and foremost, he was a great football player. He was skilful, he was fast and he could take people on and beat them, and he knew it. In training I was always jokingly (actually, half-jokingly) telling him to pass the ball a bit more. I remember one particular occasion.

'Glenn, I'm free,' I shouted at him. 'Give me the ball.'

'Oh, it's you again, is it, Ten Caat?' he answered. 'It's you on my back again.'

So he picked the ball up and drop-kicked it 100 yards away.

'This is my pass to you, Theo,' he said. 'Go and collect the ball and then you cannot complain anymore.'

It was all in good fun and we were laughing but I don't think the coach was particularly amused.

There was another time he said that he wanted to show me something on his car. So we went to the car park and there were five big guys standing round it. We stopped a little way away so they couldn't see us and he told me that they were watching his car for him. He said they were his friends, so I told him that the only reason he had friends was because he was loaded. They just wanted to share his money with him.

'Yeah, but they're good guys,' he said.

'If you lose all your money tomorrow,' I told him, 'they're gone.'

'Well maybe,' he said, 'but they're helping me out with my car because it's a really expensive car.'

Then he said, 'I'm going to start the car.'

'What do you mean you're going to start the car?' We were about 50 yards away.

'I can do that with my key,' he said, laughing.

He pushed a button on his key fob and the engine started running. The guys watching his car jumped back, wondering what on Earth was going on. They were looking all round but there was nobody else there.

'I can also sound the horn,' he said and pressed another button. Sure enough, the horn sounded. It was a big loud horn, not just a normal hooter like most cars had, this one really belted out. The five bodyguards jumped into the air and just looked scared. There they were, standing there looking after a car that suddenly burst into life on its own. I mean, if he was acting like that in Arnhem, I can't imagine what he was like in London after he joined Arsenal …!

Don't get me wrong, Glenn is a lovely guy. He was just Glenn Helder, Glenn is Glenn. He was also a showman. He's now an accomplished musician and has gained a reputation as a drummer. He always had a sense of rhythm. He and one or two of the others would always be knocking beats on the table during our team meals together. They would be banging their fingers on the table, never missing a beat. It was a talent.

I was only at Vitesse for the one season. I knew I wasn't a favourite of Herbert Neumann, although I got on okay with him. We had some interesting conversations about pretty much everything, as he was a philosopher, wanted to save the world.

That's impossible, of course, because people keep doing stupid things and act in stupid ways, but that's the kind of guy he was. In my opinion he could have become a really good football manager, but he was too emotional. To be successful in that line of work emotion is good, of course, but you also have to be a bit businesslike and a bit ruthless.

He said something very interesting to me at the end of the season. We were having a conversation and when I got up to leave his office he said to me that some people are travellers and when they're travellers you have to let them go. You have to let them go and find their own way, their own path. It's no good holding them back, they'll just become unhappy, and with that unhappiness comes resentment.

'Theo,' he said, 'you're a traveller. You want to go, you want to explore, see what else is out there for you. Who am I to hold you back? If you want to go, then go.'

When I closed the door he said, 'And by the way, I don't need you anyway!'

Twente and Veendam Encore

'Theo, I have a problem,' he said, 'and
the problem is you.'

ISSY TEN Donkelaar was the manager when I re-signed for FC Twente, but he didn't last too long. The dressing room was divided into two groups. There was one group with me and another of our midfielders, Michel Boerebach, and there was another group with Jan van Halst and Nico-Jan Hoogma. The previous season, Jan van Halst had been left out of the team because for whatever reason, and I don't know what it was, Issy ten Donkelaar preferred to play without him. If that was his decision to do so, then as a manager he's perfectly entitled to do that. His big mistake, however, was to go back on that decision after a while and reinstate him.

There was also something going on that wasn't quite right because the radio reporters seemed to know who would be in the first team at the weekend before us players did! The standard procedure was that every Friday we would have a training session before the game at the weekend and it also seemed that standard procedure was for the local radio and television guys to know exactly what the teams tactics were!

So, with all this going on, we had the two groups in the dressing room and it got to the point where the manager just had to sort things out. Ten Donkelaar and his assistant Fred Rutten gathered everybody together for a team talk.

'Boys, we've got a problem,' he said, 'and we have to do something about it. Let's have a chat and I'll let you decide what we can do to make things better.'

He and Fred then left the dressing room. I don't really know why he did that. You can't just let the players make the decisions. The group led by Jan van Halst wanted to get rid of him, but they needed everyone to be unanimous. Being one of the most experienced and senior players there at the time, I stood up and had my say.

'No way am I saying I want the coach out,' I told everyone. 'I don't want anything to do with this. I do not want it going into the papers that the players don't want to work with Issy ten Donkelaar anymore, because then that stains my name as well.'

A bit of an argument broke out with the players discussing it among ourselves. Van Halst and Hoogma wanted him out but myself and Boerebach said that it was the board that should decide what happens to the manager and not us. It isn't our place to do so. Our opinion was that we should just get on with our job and to leave those sorts of discussions to the directors of the club. We should just be training and playing and doing our best for whoever is in charge. If the board of directors want to make the change, that's their business. If Issy ten Donkelaar feels he wants to resign, that's his business. Our business was just to get on with playing.

Ten Donkelaar stayed on as manager at that point, although just a month later he was fired. Whether he decided that enough was enough or whether something else happened, I don't know, but he was gone. It was a shame but at least it was their decision and not at the hands of the players. I really stood firm on that at the time. I really didn't want to be involved in a situation where the playing staff are influencing whether management should be sacked. That to me is just wrong. That's not our responsibility or our task. Our task is to train hard and to play as well as we can on the pitch to help the team get results and points.

Fred Rutten took temporary charge for a couple of weeks before Hans Meyer was appointed as the new manager after the winter break. He was as hard as stone. As a player he was a defender and had been a league champion in East Germany with Carl Zeiss Jena before the reunification. He went on to manage the club and led them to three cup victories.

Michel Boerebach was the captain at the time but, unfortunately for him, he became the first casualty of the new manager's reign. It seems that Boerebach wasn't the type of player that Hans Meyer wanted in his team. Before the second half of the season got up and running again, we played a friendly match and Michel was on the bench. At half-time, Hans Meyer told him he was putting him on for the second half and tried to give him the captain's armband. Michel didn't like this and threw the armband back into the manager's face, saying that he didn't want to be the captain in these circumstances. He never wore the armband again and he soon left the club. Nico-Jan Hoogma was made captain in his place and the team played some good football for the rest of that season.

The following pre-season there was a bit of transfer activity as Hans Meyer began to make the team his own. Aside from Michel Boerebach, Michael Mols, who went on to play for Rangers, left the club and was replaced by Johnny Bosman. Erik ten Hag, who went on to manage Ajax and Manchester United, also came in, as did Rob McKinnon from Motherwell. Another player who joined the squad was a young Jan Vennegoor of Hesselink, who was just starting his career. His very long surname, incidentally, comes from the fact that a couple of hundred years ago there was a marriage between the Vennegoor family and the Hesselink family and, due to the prestige of both families, the married couple kept both surnames. The 'of' in his name is actually the Dutch word meaning 'or' rather than to specify a place where he comes from.

There was an amusing incident in a pre-season friendly game that we had against Barcelona. All the big names were playing for Barça that day – Vitor Baia, Pep Guardiola, Michael Reiziger, Hristo Stoichkov, Luis Enrique – and we were told that we weren't allowed to swap shirts. Nowadays you can keep everything and you often see players throwing their shirts into the crowd as well, but it was different back then. Even though we had been told that, I had already decided before the game that I would swap shirts. If they wanted to give me a fine, then okay, but I was going to swap. Hans Meyer told us that we needed to keep the shirts for the match at the weekend.

After the game, which Barcelona won 1-0, I went up to one of the defenders, to be honest I can't remember who it was as there were no names on the back of the shirts, and asked to swap shirts with him, which he did without a problem. When I got back into the dressing room I was the only one who had exchanged shirts because all the others listened to what the manager had said beforehand. I was given a hard time because of it.

'To be honest,' I answered, 'I do listen if people are talking sense to me, but not being allowed to swap shirts today made no sense to me and that's why I did it.'

I also gave my reasoning.

'We play for FC Twente, so how many games do we play against a top international team like Barcelona? Is it once a season or once in your lifetime?'

'Well,' said Meyer, 'Theo just ignored orders again so we can do one of two things. Firstly, we could order a complete new set of 20 shirts and Theo has to pay for everything.'

'But I only exchanged one shirt so we only need to order one new shirt in,' I interjected. 'I have no problem buying a replacement shirt.'

'No, Theo, that's not the case, the problem is that you don't listen,' he continued. 'You need to buy a whole new set. The other option is that we all swap shirts with Barcelona now.'

The time it took him to say that we could all swap shirts until the room emptied as all the other players ran towards the Barcelona dressing room was about two seconds! They barely let him finish his sentence before they were off. The two of us were left in there, so we just sat down and were laughing and laughing.

Hans Meyer got us playing some really good football. He really liked the technical aspect of the game, so those kind of players, myself included, were doing really well and producing some good stuff. We were one of the best teams in the league that season and picked up some really good results. At one point we went on a run where we were only beaten once in 13 matches, winning the other 12. When we got to the last six weeks of the season we were in a chase for the title with Ajax, PSV and Feyenoord. We then lost a couple of games and I remember having a talk with the manager about what was going wrong.

'The attacking players have gone off the boil,' he said to me. 'They've stopped performing as they had been.'

The thing is, and I still believe it to be the case, at that point Jan van Halst had come back into the team after a long injury lay-off and in my eyes this had disturbed the balance of the team and the rhythm that we had got into up to then. With Jan back in the line-up we started playing a little bit more defensively. This was the basis of my argument in my discussion with Hans Meyer. I said to him that the more defensive players were now starting to do the job of the attacking players, who were now not getting the ball as much. My opinion was that they had to get it and then play it forward to us and we could then get the attacks going again. That was, after all, our job in the team. He listened to my point of view but, unfortunately as it turned out, didn't change anything, maybe because of his good relationship with Jan van Halst. As a result, we only won three of the last eight games and finished the season in third place, with PSV becoming champions.

The next season I became, for only a short period, the captain of the team. It was a nice honour for me but it turned out not to be all that I expected. There were some good bits and I enjoyed having some in-depth talks with the coaching staff. As I've said a couple of times already, in Holland there was a lot more discussion between the coaches and the players. It wasn't unknown for Hans Meyer to ask me to make a line-up for the next match.

'Who are you going to play?' he would ask. 'What formation are you going to use?'

So, I would write a line-up on his whiteboard and then we would talk in depth about the team I had picked. We would talk about my choices and who our opponents' team was likely to be, what tactics they would probably use and how we would counteract them. Who were their danger men? How could we nullify their threat? What would we do when we broke away? Would we stretch their defence or trust our centre-forward one on one against their central defender? Those kinds of things. That doesn't mean, of course, that the team I was picking would actually be the team for the match, but that's what would happen. Hans Meyer was brilliant at this, particularly with the older, more experienced players. It would happen in training sessions, too.

'You and you – you pick a team,' he would say. 'Go together, sit down and talk about it and come back and pick a team.'

That's how he would get us to think tactically. If we pick this player, he isn't particularly quick so we can't press too far forward because he's always going to be a bit late getting back because the other players are faster. If I run 20 yards, he's only running 15. You had to think about all these kinds of issues. Early in the week leading up to a game the opponents' team would be written down on the board in the dressing room so we were thinking how to play against them all week, rather than wait until the day before the game to decide how to overcome our personal on-field battles. We were always thinking about our opponents' strengths, how they liked to play, any little tricks that they liked to try to do, etc. Do we try to take them on their right foot or left foot? Are they tall or short? Are they quick or slow on the turn? We tried to get as much of that in our heads as possible. Every time we went into the dressing room, it would be to re-emphasise what we needed to do.

The thing is, though, on the down side, when I was captain I didn't have a particularly tight group around me. Ideally, an entire team group would all pull together and all help one another. We had a group of younger players who were all fine, but then we also had the more experienced players, the ones who are a bit more confident in themselves, sort of working against me a bit. That's how I felt it was, anyway. I don't mean they were rebelling and arguing and that sort of thing but, for example, if I was taking the lads through their warm-down recovery training after matches, if I said to them that we were doing four lots of runs, they would do three. Those are the little tricks that I'm talking about. It seems that they wanted to test me out a bit. The ironic thing here is that Erik ten Hag was in this group, and from what I know of him as a coach at Ajax and Manchester United, he would have stood for none of that nonsense there!

After a while I got fed up with all these sorts of things happening and I told Hans Meyer that I didn't want to be the captain anymore. Thinking back, that was a big mistake that I made. I should have stuck it out and talked to those players about it. After all, it was the manager who had made me the captain and, in reality, they were being cheeky towards him rather than me with their behaviour. I should have played it a bit harder.

'I'm sick of this,' I said to him. 'If the players don't want me to be captain, then I don't want to be captain. It's like playtime at school with the children who are just doing whatever they want to do.'

Strangely enough, I detected that Hans Meyer was actually quite pleased at my decision, I could see it in his eyes. I think he wanted to make Nico-Jan Hoogma captain again and couldn't really strip me of the armband because he'd only just made me the captain.

During that season we all went off for a training camp in Gran Canaria in the winter break. We were playing in a little friendly tournament while we were over there and, after the pre-match meal before we played the German team Wolfsburg, Hans Meyer asked everyone if they were going to sleep before the match, and then he specifically asked me. I told him no, I don't always sleep before games, and he said, in that case, could I sit down with him as he wanted to speak with me.

'Theo, I have a problem,' he said, 'and the problem is you.'

'Excuse me?' I asked. I wasn't really expecting that.

'You're interfering with how the team is performing,' he informed me, 'and you're not playing as well as you did before.'

I told him what the problem was. 'It's the tactics,' I said. 'We're not playing as a team, as a unit. With Rico Steinmann playing it unbalances things a little and we have 4-4-2 with the two strikers. We need to be playing 4-3-3. The way we're playing now isn't working.'

Steinmann had been signed in pre-season from FC Köln in Germany. The funny thing was, exactly what I said to him about the problems with how he currently wanted us to play then happened in the match against Wolfsburg. Steinmann was playing too deep, I couldn't get on the ball, Johnny Bosman couldn't get on the ball. At some point during the game, I pointed this out to him.

'There you are,' I said, 'you can see it with your own eyes. You need to do something about it.' But nothing happened. So, what I decided to do, and maybe in hindsight it might not have been the greatest idea, was to just wait and see how often I would get the ball. I carried on doing my job, offensively and defensively, but I stopped actually asking for the ball. For the rest of the game I hardly touched it. The match ended 0-0 and was decided by a penalty shoot-out. Normally, I would be one of the ones who would take a penalty but he didn't let me this time. We won the shoot-out and went through to the final.

The next morning, after we had all had breakfast together, Hans Meyer stood up at the table and said to me in no uncertain terms that he wasn't happy and that I wouldn't be playing anymore, only training. And that's what happened. We played the final, which we won, but I wasn't even a substitute. Normally, the players who weren't chosen to be part of the squad would still be there sitting on or near the bench, but not me. I was sitting behind the goal, not really paying much attention to what was going on. It was obvious that the manager didn't want me, or at least didn't trust me at this point, and I wasn't in his plans. I called my wife during that match and spoke to her for most of it. And that was pretty much it, he hardly used me again at all.

At the airport after the training camp, with all the players wandering around trying to kill time before the flight back to Holland, I saw Hans Meyer sitting at a table so I took my cup of coffee and went to sit with him. This was after there had been a fair bit of silence between us and surely he couldn't just ignore me here – that would just be a bit too obvious.

'Hello coach,' I said, 'can we talk?'

This time he couldn't ignore me and we did have a chat and aired our various opinions, and he started playing me again. To be fair to him, he was fine with me as we were speaking one on one. I told him what I thought about things and he told me what he thought about things. Fortunately, I'm the type of guy who has no problem talking as two adults and I can leave the emotion out of it and, at that point, I thought that enough was enough anyway and we had to have a talk together. We had a decent chat about many things, not only football, and cleared the air a little bit. Despite that, though, the warning signs were there and in the following season, my last at the club, it got even worse.

In all the four years I played with FC Twente in my second stint there, we always had groups of players rather than one big, united squad. I also have the feeling that Hans Meyer was playing with people, testing them out in one way or another. This meant that the atmosphere in the dressing room wasn't always that good, which is a bad thing in itself. At one point I found myself throwing a cup of tea over one particular player and then going into the medical room to calm myself down. Those kinds of things happened. Some of the players seemed to revel in it but I was one of those who didn't want to get involved in those sorts of games. I was there to play football and be part of a team. I do think Hans Meyer enjoyed it. I think he liked making decisions and manoeuvring certain people into certain positions just to see what would happen. He would leave people out of the team for a while just to gauge their reaction. This is what he did with me during my last season there. In the training sessions I was always one of the better players but, when it came to the matchdays, he stopped playing me.

For the 1998/99 season, Rob McKinnon had gone back to Scotland with Hearts and Nico-Jan Hoogma left for Hamburg. Hans wanted to play with a lot of younger players and, along with Jan van Halst and Erik ten Hag, the three of them seemed to be very close and appeared to work things out a lot between them. A few young Belgian players were brought in, which ultimately proved to be a bit of a problem for me.

Our first league game was against Heerenveen and we lost 1-0. During that game I also got injured midway through the first half. One of the new Belgian players, Kurt Van De Paar, took my place. I was missing for a couple of weeks and when I got back I was very much in and out of the side, being substituted and even playing at left-back on occasions. Van De Paar became a regular in the matchday squad and eventually Hans Meyer decided that he would be one of his new favourites, and I was frozen out.

It was also round about that time that, for some reason, it became a thing for all of the players to walk around the pitch after every game and applaud the fans. Who came up with this idea, I don't know. I always felt a bit awkward doing this, especially if the team hadn't played particularly well. There was one occasion where we played away at NEC Nijmegen. I was on the bench for the game and didn't get on and, even though I hadn't played, I still had to go through the post-match warm-down routine. When it was all done, with the other players applauding and thanking the supporters, I went straight to the dressing room. Jan van Halst was the next one in after me, followed by Erik ten Hag. They were both angry at me and telling me how I should have been waving to the public and that they wanted to teach me a lesson.

'If you were in my shoes,' I said to them, 'a player in his 30s who has done his best for the club for three years and now, because there's a bit of a problem between me and the coach, he makes me do that ridiculous warm-down even though I haven't played in the game, what would you think? It's a joke. I'm not accepting it and I'm not accepting this from you, either. So shut up, take a shower and leave me alone.'

Jan and Erik liked to take on responsibility, in fact overly so. When I was the captain I was responsible for a few things. I would do little speeches for the sponsors and talk to some of the players, and if the coach asked me to do something then I would do that, but I wasn't really a player who would stand in the dressing room in front of everybody else and tell them what they needed to do and what would happen if they didn't. I did my job, of course, but I was quite easy-going. Jan and Erik, though, were the opposite of my character. It seemed that they wanted to control everything. In my opinion, if that's how you're going to go about things, then you're just looking for enemies. The three of us had a big argument in the dressing room after that match. I also told Hans Meyer that it was daft I had to do it as I hadn't got on and, as one of the senior members of the playing staff, he was treating me like a child and I wasn't going to accept it anymore.

The last discussion I had with Hans Meyer was after a cup game against Fortuna Sittard. Again I was substitute and watched on as Fortuna went into half-time 5-1 up. I went on for the second half and, in my opinion, did okay. I wasn't brilliant but played what I thought was a normal game. I can't change things all on my own, of course, and needed my team-mates, who had been taken apart in the first half, to step up. The match finished 5-2 but afterwards the manager put a lot of the blame for the loss on me. He said that the chairman was complaining about me and that one or two of the sponsors were a bit annoyed, and this was my fault and that was my fault. He said to me that the chairman had asked him, 'Why do you play Ten Caat?' and that he couldn't accept these kinds of performances from me.

I know I can be awkward at certain times, but this wasn't one of them. I genuinely played that game in the proper way. If your team is 5-1 down at half-time, how can you possibly blame the substitute who only went on for the second half? The game was already lost.

After our next training session following that game, he came up to me again, saying that we needed to talk. He then said to me that I was doing it on purpose. He actually accused me of playing badly deliberately. I couldn't believe he would say that.

'You're always the best player in the training sessions,' was his argument, 'and that's how I want to see you play in the games.'

'I do my best,' I told him, 'but if you're not going to change your tactics then it isn't going to work. We've already had the discussion, more than once, and I've already told you that it's not my type of game that you've started to play. I do my best but the way we play now is so defensive that I cannot possibly make such a difference during the matches. In the training sessions you see what I can do.'

'You're going to have to play with the reserves until the end of the season,' was his answer.

'Well, if that's your decision then that's your decision,' I said. He had made his mind up and there was nothing I could do.

I joined up with the reserves for a couple of months and then one day suddenly, out of the blue, I was back training with the first team again. After that session he asked me to come to his office and he told me that he was planning on playing me against Vitesse the following weekend. The thing is, I knew that the first team had a few injuries and that was the reason he was recalling me.

'This cannot just be a one-off thing,' I said to him. 'It isn't fair if you put me back into the group again but only for one game. If you want me back in the first-team squad then, yes, I'll train and play with you again, but not just for one single game.'

Hans Meyer knew what my stand was on this, and I didn't think this was unreasonable. It wasn't fair to me if I was in the first-team squad for one match then back in the reserves, then back with the first team if they needed me again, and it also wasn't fair for the coaches of the reserves. So, after the last training session before the match, he spoke with me again and said that he had thought about the situation and that he wouldn't be taking me back with the first team permanently.

'Then I'm not going to play,' I told him. 'You can fine me if you wish, you can go to the chairman and I'll tell him my side of the story if he'll listen, but I'm not going to play. I know I have to work to get my money but, from my point of view, you've already treated me badly and now you tell me this. I'm sorry but I'm not going to play just because you've got a few injured players.'

That was in the April of the season and I didn't play for Twente again. My contract still had an option for another year but Veendam came in for me and offered me a pretty good wage to join them for a second division team, so I signed. Three weeks later, Jan van Halst also left Twente to join Ajax.

Funnily enough, we had a pre-season friendly against Twente. When we arrived for the game I had a long conversation with Hans Meyer.

'Well, Theo,' he said, 'we decided three weeks too early.'

Those were his exact words. He said he was sorry at the way it ended because, up until it all went sour, we actually had a really good relationship, Hans and I. The last few months obviously were pretty bad but, even then, when we were talking about something other than my place in the team, be it other players or tactics or just discussing life, it was still okay.

'To be honest, Theo,' he said, 'I miss you.'

'I miss you, too,' I told him, 'but I'm playing for Veendam now.'

'It's a shame you came to an agreement three weeks too soon,' he acknowledged.

He knew what the real problem was. Nowadays I don't have any problem at all with those guys, but at the time when it's your life and your career, things can obviously get a bit more strained. It was nice that he said that but also a little strange. It just shows how bad the situation had been allowed to get. Then, just weeks into the new season, Hans Meyer went back to Germany with Borussia Mönchengladbach.

Rejoining Veendam was one of the biggest mistakes of my career. Everybody makes mistakes, and that was one of mine. I should never have left Twente, I should have ended my career there. At some point at Veendam I was blamed for practically everything. Azing Griever was the coach and he desperately wanted to lead the team back up into the Eredivisie. Before I signed, I had a meeting with him and listened to the plan that he had for the team, and it looked pretty good. He said he wanted me to play in the centre of midfield as a playmaker behind two strikers and I was up for it. So what happened? For the first pre-season friendly he played 4-4-2 with me wide on the left.

'What are you doing?' I asked Griever after the game. 'This is not what we talked about.'

'Ah, yes,' he said, 'but in this situation it's best for the team.'

'But I didn't come here to play in this position,' I told him. 'I want to play behind the strikers, setting things up for them.'

It was to no avail. I had to play on the wing. Of course, I did my best but it just wasn't what I expected or what I wanted.

I had been playing for 15 years at the top level and was now in the second division playing for a coach who told me one thing to get me to sign and then did another thing after I joined. Not only that, it was a noticeably lower level. I mean absolutely no disrespect to my team-mates here, but I would be playing the same type of passes as I had been at Aberdeen and Twente and Groningen, but now some of them weren't getting to the players because they were that little bit slower. I can't blame them, it wasn't their fault, they were all trying their best, but it was a lower standard. Also, on the other side of it, when it was me making the forward runs, I had been used in my career to receiving seven out of ten passes, now it was two or three. The game began to flow away from me and it was getting harder to make a meaningful contribution. I had many talks with the manager about this situation, telling him that from the position he was playing me there wasn't much I could do to change things round and to have a more influential impact on matches. I told him I needed to be in the centre of midfield, where he said he was going to play me anyway.

On one occasion I had a bit of an altercation with one of the other players. I didn't mean it to go that way but I offered him a bit of advice, maybe criticised him a little too harshly perhaps, and we got into an argument. The next day I was in the players' lounge having a coffee and he and a bunch of others were also sitting there. I said 'good morning boys' but they didn't say a word. They completely blanked me. My attitude was that what happened yesterday was yesterday and now it was forgotten. Now it seemed that instead of having a problem with one player, I was having a problem with six players. That was the environment there.

A little while into my second season, Azing Griever was replaced as coach by Martin Koopman, with whom I had played at FC Twente during my first stint there. Martin Koopman's managerial career has taken him all over the place. As well as Holland, he has taken positions in Saudi Arabia, China, Aruba, Ghana and the Maldives, where he worked with Rene Hiddink, the brother of Guus Hiddink.

During that period I would always wear a hat – if it rained I would have my hat on. It was just one of those things. Throughout my career I would go through patches of doing a certain thing for a few months and then stopping and then starting doing something else a little while later. A lot of players do that, I don't really know why. So, at this point, I was going through a stage of wearing a hat. The local newspaper asked Martin Koopman why I was wearing a hat during training when it was seven or eight degrees. For some reason it became big news. I mean, seriously. Is it really that big a story, 'Footballer Wears Hat'? Maybe because we weren't playing so well they decided to concentrate on other things, but surely there must have been bigger news than Theo ten Caat wearing a hat!

Eventually Koopman stopped playing me and started leaving me on the bench. I remember our conversation …

'I can't play you, Theo,' he said. 'I'm sorry but you're just not good enough anymore.'

That isn't the sort of thing any footballer ever wants to hear. I do think, however, that he didn't give me a chance because this started within the first month of his appointment. For a while I was in and out but then it became more out than in, so 2001/02, my third and last season at Veendam and my final season in professional football, was terrible. I was being used as a scapegoat, getting the blame for every single thing that went wrong. They seemed to have no respect for me and I wasn't enjoying it anymore. I felt so out of things that I didn't even go to the end-of-season party.

That was it for me, I decided to stop. I was 37 at the time and didn't need to take any rubbish anymore. I was still fit and thought I could do a job, but mentally it was just so frustrating. All the circumstances just drained my enthusiasm and it felt like the right time to quit. If you don't have fun anymore in what you're doing, whatever it is, then it's time to look elsewhere. I was going to training knowing that I wouldn't be playing at the weekend and there just was no point. So, yeah, that was when Theo ten Caat signed off from professional football.

Football Then and Football Now

*In the world today, and it isn't just in football,
money is the reason why you make choices even if
those choices are not good ones.*

THE BIGGEST difference between football now and when I was playing is the professionalism of it all. You could read that statement in two different ways. You could read it and think, *Well there you are then, it's more professional now so therefore it must be a better product.* Or you could look at it in the way that perhaps a bit of the fun has gone from the game.

When I joined FC Twente they had the club manager, head coach, the assistant coach who was also in charge of the reserves, the secretary, the accountant, and the kit man who was also the physio. An organisation of seven or eight people was normal at the time. Now you've got 300 people! On the playing staff there was the first team and there was the second team and no more. Again, you could look at that both ways. You might be convinced that having big organisations with hundreds of people doing hundreds of jobs makes sure that everything is done properly and everyone and everything is working to full capacity. On the other hand, you might think that's a bit too clinical, that the fun has been squeezed out. That's a matter of personal opinion, of course, and will differ depending on your mindset and probably your age.

One thing that nobody could surely argue against is that there's far too much football shown on the television. You might think that it's great that you can watch virtually any game you want to, but it becomes an overload. It used to be that it would be a bit of an event if your favourite team was playing live on TV and you would definitely try to make a point to watch it, but now it's all over the place. It isn't as exciting anymore and that could lead to a lack of enthusiasm for the game because it's now so commonplace. In Holland only the bigger teams like Ajax, PSV or Feyenoord would be shown on television because they had a lot of supporters, but even they weren't on all the time. Now even the lower league teams are live on television. The only reason for this can be money.

The first stage of all of this was when somebody came up with the idea of advertising all around the pitch, and the clubs then started thinking that they had to make special room in their stadiums for the sponsors, give them executive boxes and rooms inside the stadiums where they could go. Let's also give them the opportunity to buy shares in the club as well. So then we started having not only the real football supporters in for the games, but businessmen for networking as well. It started becoming more of a circus. There they are talking to people and trying to take something out of the game. The VIPs became more and more important and gained more and more power because if the club needed more money they would go to the sponsors, so their organisations were becoming more and more important to the clubs.

Then there was shirt sponsoring. When I started out nobody had sponsorship across the front of the shirts, now everybody has it. Some teams have more than one. Barcelona tried to hold out and not have a sponsor – I think their reasoning was they didn't want anything to spoil the shirt – but even they eventually gave way. Then you started getting the players' names on the shirts so the kids could go out and buy one with their favourite player on. It's all about how much money can be made out of merchandising, how much money can be made out of sponsoring. Football always was, and in my opinion always should be, for the ordinary people, but now it's being used by the money-makers.

There are even a lot of clubs listed on the Stock Exchange. And in the last few years it has even gone further than that with the megarich tycoons from the Middle East, who made big money out of oil and whatever, coming in to own clubs like Paris Saint-Germain and Manchester City. Some businessmen even have franchises, owning a football club in the UK, a baseball team in America, and so on.

I know this is the way that football has gone but it's moving away from the real supporters. There's no way to stop it now, it has gone too far. It's the snowball effect – it just rolls on and on, getting bigger and bigger. The only way it will finish is in a big crash.

Another effect of all this money in the game and all the wheeling and dealing is that you see players who play for 10 or 15 clubs during their career. Clubs are more often now taking a gamble on players than they used to. Manchester United bought Antony from Ajax for £80m. Is he really worth that money? He played well in Holland and not everybody who is a decent player can play well in Holland. Clubs buy and buy and buy young kids of 16, 17, 18 years, and if only one succeeds, then all well and good. They can make money out of that player but all the other ones can either go back to where they came from or are shipped out to other clubs.

When the Bosman ruling came into being it changed football big-time. When the ruling became law I was personally affected. Before then we were owned by our clubs. Depending on your age, your annual salary was multiplied by a certain number and that was the transfer fee. If another team would pay that amount, then the transfer could happen, but if they weren't willing to pay that amount of money, then the club who owned you could refuse to do business and that was the end of that. If you wanted to walk away from the club, the only possible way you could do that was to join an amateur team and stay there for a couple of years before trying to get back into professional football again.

I was caught out with that. As I've said elsewhere, I spent three years at Twente and then there was a problem with the board and the offer that they made me to stay, which was a disaster for me financially and I had no real option but to leave the club. When you reached the age of 32 under the old system you were entitled to a free transfer without being blocked by the transfer system. The ironic thing is that when I became 32 and thought that I at last had the opportunity to make some big money, that's when the Bosman ruling kicked in! Isn't that typical? Now anybody whose contract was up, no matter how old they were, was entitled to a free transfer, but I, at 32, was already entitled to one! I could have made some serious money then but Bosman ruined everything for me!

When the Bosman ruling came in the whole landscape of football changed. Now that the players were free to go whenever they wanted to, the clubs had to react to that as well. They had to figure a way to make money out of the players before they left. The players' agents became more important. Suddenly, if they had a player that was really talented and did a good job for them over two or three years, they had to get them to sign a new contract. If not, they had to be sold off for fear that they would leave for nothing. Clubs and agents are now working so closely together. Apparently, according to FIFA, in the year 2023, clubs spent over £700m on agents' fees, so that's obviously an issue.

It was put forward that football players were slaves before Bosman, but I think they're more slaves now because the agents have so much power. Players like Messi and Ronaldo don't need agents – they've got them but they don't need them – because they sell themselves, but other players go from one club to another so frequently. In my day transfers didn't happen half as much as they do now. Nowadays clubs are hiring players, not only to improve their team, but also with a view to selling them on in a couple of years for a big profit. Which is fine by the agents because the more players they sell the more money they make.

As a knock-on effect we now have UEFA and FIFA thinking about money all the time and not necessarily, in my opinion, what's best for the game. You can add the owners of clubs into this, as well. Why on Earth would you go over to Saudi Arabia to play a Barcelona vs Real Madrid game? Yes, the people of Saudi Arabia want to see those teams, of course, but that's not the reason it's decided to play a game there. If that's the reason then why aren't they bringing these teams over to where I live in the north-east of Holland, to show the people there? Or why aren't they taking them to the Scottish Highlands, because I'm sure those people would like to see Barcelona and Madrid rock up into town. No. But if you play somewhere that can give you $50m into your bank account, then that's a much more attractive option, isn't it? In the world today, and it isn't just in football, money is the reason why you make choices, even if those choices aren't good ones.

Here in Holland, because of the Champions League, it's only the top three that make real money. The gap between the top three – Ajax, PSV and Feyenoord – and the rest is getting bigger and bigger and bigger. Look at Celtic and Rangers in Scotland. Okay, they never do anything much in the Champions League, but year after year they're playing in Europe and getting the money from it. That's why they can afford to pay five times as much for a player than the other Scottish clubs can, and also hold out for massive fees, in comparison with everybody else, when selling players. Celtic received £25m from Arsenal for Kieran Tierney, Rangers got £20m when Calvin Bassey joined Ajax, whereas Aberdeen's highest fee ever received is just over £4m from Liverpool for Calvin Ramsey. The television companies are only interested in the two Glasgow clubs as well, and then there was talk of them joining the English Premier League, which was just a joke. The Premier League has nothing to do with them. If they want to play against the English teams then they need to arrange friendlies or get drawn against them in Europe.

Then there's the European Super League that they keep talking about. Surely nobody believes that money isn't the only motivator behind that. If it ever happens, and I hope it doesn't, it's only for the big teams to make more and more money, meaning that the balance gets even worse in the national leagues. It's the rich looking after themselves. Bayer Leverkusen are currently doing well in Germany but the big teams will always be Bayern Munich and Dortmund. Every so often in Spain they have a certain team rising up to challenge Barcelona and Real Madrid – teams like Valencia, Atlético Madrid, Sevilla, Athletic Bilbao have all had a go – but those two will always be the big two.

What also happened after the Bosman ruling was freedom of movement between countries. I'm not saying this is necessarily a bad thing, of course, because I moved from Holland to Scotland, but it really did open the floodgates. Not only did it change the transfer rules nationally but it also called into question freedom of movement between countries in the European Union. When that part of it got looked into more, teams realised they didn't have to stick to two or three foreigners in their first-team line-up and international transfers became a thing that happened every day. Before that, with limited squad places open for foreign players, the buying teams had to make sure they were getting quality rather than just quantity. As a consequence, a lot of football nations are losing their own traditional identity a bit because of all the different cultures coming together. Again, I'm not saying freedom of movement is a bad thing, merely that I find it interesting what has happened because of it. The Dutch people are arrogant and have a big mouth, the English think they rule the world, Scotland is happy to beat England, everyone hates the Germans (of course we don't hate the Germans, we're all just jealous of their success!), the French are very artistic but not up to the battle, all Brazilians play samba football, etc., you see what I mean? Traditional stereotypes, but are any of them actually so anymore?

The big realisation of what could happen with big-money international transfers started with the three Dutchmen – Ruud Gullit, Frank Rijkaard and Marco van Basten – when they went over to AC Milan and helped them become the best team in the world. Of course, there were individuals who became stars abroad in the years before, such as Maradona, Michel Platini, Gary Lineker, players like this, but the boom definitely came after Bosman. We then started getting a lot of young Brazilians coming over to Holland, like Romário and Ronaldo, to develop themselves in the Dutch league because the Dutch league was pretty good at that time.

It's funny that, with all the moving around there is, it always seems to be the local boys who are the favourites. They get their name sung: 'He's one of our own.'

It would be interesting to see what would happen if they brought in some kind of transfer budget like they have in America. They're all allowed to spend a certain amount of money and they can spend it how they like. You can buy one or two stars, you can buy 50 players, as long as you stay within budget. If they do that they have to be creative, they have to think, and can't just go to agents and make deals where we buy this player and then sell him off again in a couple of years' time, etc. It's never going to happen like that, of course, because the culture and way of thinking would have to change completely, but it would certainly make things a little bit more interesting.

Having some form of budget would also be good for the youth development because that would become more important. More money would be spent on that because it would be important for clubs to develop their own players due to the budget restrictions. The easiest way to have a sensible salary budget is to get players from your own youth system instead of recruiting them from another team. You would also then start to get your own culture back because there would be more local players to whom the team would mean more. Every team used to have its own culture, its own feel, rather than just being another football team whose players have been gathered from anywhere they could get hold of someone.

There does seem to be an awful lot of changes to the laws of the game now, as well. Every season something has to be tweaked or changed for no apparent reason. Do all these changes make the game better? Of course not. Which brings me to VAR. It has certainly had its critics since it was introduced. What I will say for video assistant referee is that you have five people watching the matches on various screens and if somebody gives somebody else an elbow at the other end of the pitch from where the play is happening, it gets noticed, which can only be a good thing. In my day nobody would have seen it. But even with VAR there are questionable things. The guy who is sitting behind the television screen is a person as well, just like the on-field referee, and he has his own interpretation of what he has seen and, actually, is it really that bad that referees make mistakes? Even with handballs in the penalty box, there will always be discussions about what was accidental or not, or whether the player was able to get out of the way or not. It's got to the point where now you see defenders defending with their hands behind their back. That's just ridiculous, worrying that much that the ball will hit their arm and they will give away a penalty. They then don't have the right balance, their movement isn't what it should be and there's no way they can defend properly. In my day it was a penalty when you obviously moved your hand towards the ball to gain an advantage.

Marco van Basten got it right with what he said about VAR and the offside ruling. He said that as long as there's body contact or some overlapping of the bodies of the forward and the defender, no matter how far apart they may be in the width of the pitch, then there should be no offside. If there's any doubt, give it to the attacker. It should be so simple. We've seen goals disallowed because somebody's elbow or armpit has been ruled offside. I mean, seriously ...!

Has VAR made football fairer? If you look at football now and football before, watch 100 games, has it made it fairer? No, I don't think so. What it has done is taken responsibility away from the linesmen. They used to raise their flags when they thought a player was offside and the referee stopped the game to give a free kick or acknowledge the linesman but waved play on if he disagreed. Now, half the time they don't even bother waving their flag even if they might think the attacker is offside, because they know VAR will intervene anyway. The good decisions and bad decisions will even themselves out over a season and the better teams will always be the better teams that win most games anyway. They don't need – or shouldn't need – a video assistant to help them. The emotion in the game is being killed. A team scores a goal, the crowd goes crazy and then we all have to stop and wait for a VAR check. A minute or two later the goal is given but it's impossible to celebrate in the same way because all the initial excitement had been curbed.

There's also a school of thought, and a popular one, that football is getting better. I don't think football is getting better but it's definitely getting faster. I was recently watching a programme about the history of Benfica and they were featuring Eusébio. What a brilliant player he was. The best players of today are no better than Eusébio was in his time. The football now isn't better but it *is* faster, more physical and more tactical, and that's because of all the new training facilities that are available now. When I was learning the game, even when I was playing, there wasn't a huge amount of fitness training the way you would think of it now. In Holland we would train five or six times a week and then play on the Sunday.

In my opinion, and I know that many people will argue this point, the players from 40 or 50 years ago were, in general, better football players than they are now. A lot of today's game is about fitness and how to best utilise your body with what you eat and when to have rest periods, and all that sort of thing, but players like Johan Cruyff, Franz Beckenbauer, Ferenc Puskás, Alfredo di Stéfano, George Best, Bobby Charlton, Johan Neeskens, Willem van Hanegem, Denis Law, all those guys, they didn't have any of that. They were trained in a different way to how the players are trained now. Take all the dietary advancements, for example. When I was young there weren't all the vitamins and all those other things put in the food. There are so many supplements used now that the players are getting stronger. If you watch old football games it's noticeable the difference in the body weights of the players. A lot of the older guys look skinny compared to most of the players today.

Then there's the equipment. The balls are lighter now, the football boots are smaller and more flimsy, so the game is getting faster. Yes, the players are becoming stronger and faster but that doesn't make them wiser in terms of playing the game to help them to read the game better. I truly believe that if you had the best players of today playing a game against the best players of years gone past – players like the ones I've already named and others like Michel Platini, Pelé, Garrincha, those old Italian defenders like Paolo Maldini, Claudio Gentile, etc., if they were playing in their prime, I really believe the older players would win. Why? One reason. They have more brains. You really don't find very many players anymore with the footballing intelligence of people like Glenn Hoddle, Frank Rijkaard, Jean Tigana, Kenny Dalglish, Hristo Stoichkov, Daniel Passarella, who was the best defender in the world. I could go on and on.

Who today are like those guys? We have Messi and Ronaldo, and Kevin de Bruyne is a good player, Kylian Mbappe obviously has talent, Harry Kane and Erling Haaland know how to score, Martin Odegaard has good intelligence. My money is still on the old guys, though. Maybe I'm living in the past, I don't know.

If I look at football now, and I'm looking at the Dutch team, there's Virgil van Dijk, and he's one of the top players in Europe. Compare him to Beckenbauer, though, or Passarella or Bobby Moore or Alan Hansen or Willie Miller or Paolo Maldini … Really?

'Come on Beckenbauer, come on Di Stéfano, come and play with me. We're going to play a game against the guys who make 100 million a year.'

My wife tells me I live in the past but, you know, that's where it really was. I tell her, 'Look at those players, though.'

Some people say that Cristiano Ronaldo is the best player ever. I tell you what, though, George Best would just be having a laugh with him. He would run rings round him. 'Come on boy,' he would be saying, 'forget trying to beat me, tonight we'll get a taxi into town and we'll have a drink. Perhaps you could try to keep up with me there, instead ...'

Coaching and the
Theo ten Caat Academy

Maybe I should have made more mistakes in my passing and then perhaps I would have been more popular! Maybe I should have tried a little bit less!

WHAT'S POPULAR, what's in vogue, always changes in football. I know time moves on and things have become a lot more scientific now, I understand that. In the last few years everybody has started wearing high-performance garments under their football shirts that measure all sorts of data for all sorts of analysis. How far players run, the intensity of their runs, etc. is all recorded and every single little thing is broken down and analysed. Then everybody has their own personal numbers and what's good for them and what's bad for them and they're told 'you can't go over this' and 'you can't go over that' and that it's dangerous to go into the red. We didn't have any of that when I was playing.

In my day we must have all gone into the red twice a week. Nowadays, we have all the data but we also see so many players after 75 minutes going down with cramp. That never used to happen. Maybe in a cup final on a big pitch with everybody feeling a little bit more tension than usual, but not in normal league games.

So what's right and what's wrong? Players who get cramp after 75 minutes or just training as hard as you can during the week and having two days off before the game to settle down a bit? You see all these statistics after every match that this player has run however many kilometres and that player has made this number of short sprints and the number of passes that every player has made. Those sorts of things, especially the things like how many passes a player has made, can look really good but can also be quite misleading. A little pass of five yards backwards still counts as a successful pass, but which footballer on this entire planet cannot do that?

I've had players who have made a mistake and then run 30, 40, 50 yards because they have to win the ball back. When they make their challenge all the crowd are cheering for the tackle. The thing is, if he didn't make the mistake before, he wouldn't have to run 50 yards back to try to redeem himself. If you do this, though, all the crowd cheer and you're the most popular player in the team. That's how you become a popular player – make mistakes, run back, make the tackle and everyone says you're a winner. Maybe I should have made more mistakes in my passing and then perhaps I would have been more popular! Maybe I should have tried a little bit less!

I grew up watching the style of Rinus Michels, Johan Cruyff, Rob Rensenbrink, Epi Drost and people like them. The Dutch always want to attack and we always try to play an attacking system if we can; 4-3-3 was always the favoured system and I think it's still the best system to employ for youth development. If you're playing a game, you obviously want to win, but you also want to have fun. We don't play a 4-4-2 system and try to get in the angles, we want to create things and have nice build-ups and keep the ball in our possession rather than just getting it in the box as soon as possible to hit a big target man.

It sounds easy and it sounds obvious but the most important thing in football is the ball. When you're a kid you want to kick the ball around and do nice things with the ball, keeping it up in the air without letting it touch the ground, nice dribbling movements, all those sorts of things. I'm a creator, I want to make something. To score goals you have to first create chances, and they come from a good pass or a nice dribble, something creative. Not every single time, of course, but if you're proficient in these things more chances will come along. Traditionally, the Dutch are creative and we want to have fun. Attacking-wise we want to put pressure on every part of the field, we want to have the ball. We don't like the *catenaccio* that the Italians play, where they just wait and wait and wait and then counter-attack, bang bang, two passes and a shot on goal.

Rinus Michels I like a lot. I have books about him. One of his phrases is 'the habitat'. He talks about the habitat of a football player and the habitat of a dog. He came up with a story that I really like. If you take your dog out in the car to the forest and let it loose when you get there, what does it do? It goes crazy. Just goes everywhere. All over the place. The dog loves it, it just loves it, loves having the freedom. So, with young kids, you give them a football and you tell them to just go and enjoy themselves, go all over the place. Go and have fun. That dog never thinks negatively about what might happen. If you're a young football player who is still developing then you should never think negatively. When you reach a level that it's your profession then, yes, of course, you need to think a bit more about what you're doing and the effect it will have on your team. When you're growing up, though, as a kid, just go and enjoy yourself. Give them the ball and let them play. Don't say anything.

When I take my boot camps I always shout to my kids, 'Go to the ball, go to the ball,' so you get a whole group of players all running towards the ball. Conversely to that, I've heard other coaches saying to kids of seven or eight years of age, 'Move away from the ball, go into the space.' I think to myself, 'No, don't teach them that now, teach them to love the ball. Teach them how to play football first and then in the years to come bring in the tactics.'

Dennis Bergkamp said that he always wanted to play a beautiful kind of football – which he was brilliant at, incidentally – but when he went to Arsenal he had Tony Adams and Martin Keown kicking him in training, trying to toughen him up and teaching him how to look after himself more physically on a football pitch. Don't get me wrong, I have great respect for those guys, for the hard men who could really put their foot in and destroy the game if they wanted to. You do need those kind of players. Every team needs them if they want to have success. Before you get to that stage, though, that level that Bergkamp had reached, it's all about having fun. I sometimes tell my younger boys when they're playing football to pretend they're going on a holiday or an adventure, make an adventure out of it. Enjoy yourselves, laugh with each other, even when you make mistakes. Don't worry about the things that you do wrong.

Holland is a country of 17, 18 million people, and we play some really good football against countries who have so many more people than us, so many more who, just going by the relative population figures, you would think would give us a lot harder time. So we must be doing something right. It's also the way we are. The Dutch are generally a little bit arrogant, it's one of our national characteristics. I'm not trying to put anybody down here but it's true, we are. Our philosophy is to just be yourself and don't worry about others. If somebody else has another opinion, well okay, that's your opinion, and I think that sort of comes across in the way we as a nation like to play football.

I remember one occasion from my second spell at Twente. Our coach, Hans Meyer, gave his team talk before a friendly game and I totally disagreed with what he said. I took hold of the ball and I said to the boys, 'What's the first thing you want to do when you play football?' They all came back to me with some crazy answers about doing this and doing that, so I said to them, 'The first thing is to kick the ball.'

He was just looking at me, so I carried on.

'Don't listen to what he's just told you,' I said, 'that's a load of old rubbish. The only thing we're going to do is get out on to the pitch and have fun. It's a friendly game so we'll do our thing, try to attack if we can and not worry if we make a mistake. It's one of those days, boys, where it doesn't matter.'

There's so often too much pressure put on football players. The only pressure that counts is the pressure that you put on yourself, not the pressure from the press or the fans or your team-mates. Obviously, I always wanted to win every match but you have to accept that sometimes you don't win. What happens when you lose? You go home, you wake up in the morning, you have your breakfast and you get on with your life. Of course you want to win games but you have to accept that you have to lose some as well. If you're afraid of losing games, then you'll never win a game. The coach will always tell his team to go out and win the game, he would never say they should go out and try not to lose the game. It's just that way of thinking.

'Come on boys, let's go out and have fun and play our best and try to win the game.'

That's what the coach should say, it's a positive attitude.

'Come on boys, go out and try not to lose.'

It's the same message but is it a positive way of thinking? It's a completely different attitude. The way we grew up was always to look on the bright side and to have that positivity rather than have in the back of our minds that we dare not lose. Throughout my career I lost a lot of games, of course. Did it hurt? Yes. Did it make me cry? No. Did it cost me money? Yes. Did I learn from it? Not always. Did I make the same mistakes more than once? Of course I did.

The thing is, when you're a professional football player, in your mind you're still the same kid who was running around with the ball all those years before. Just look at the Holland team that won the European Championship in 1988. Creatively they were superb. They had Marco van Basten, Ruud Gullit, Frank Rijkaard, Arnold Mühren, Gerald Vanenburg, and even Ronald Koeman as a defender was brilliant creatively. A lot of talent on the ball. The only true hard-man defensive player in that team was Jan Wouters.

The coaching licence that I've got, the UEFA A Licence, is a special licence that enables me to train youth players. It takes almost a whole year of studying and doing exercises, 45 weeks of hard work. I really had to study hard for my licence. The A Licence is the level down from the UEFA Pro Licence, but with it I can coach youth teams up to the age of 18 as well as reserve teams for top-level clubs. If I had done the Senior Licence, I wouldn't have been allowed to coach the younger kids, so I chose to do the A Licence instead. Aside from all the usual football and tactical stuff, I also had to study how a 12-year-old boy may act in a certain situation and how a 14- or 15-year-old might act differently in exactly the same situation. We also had to consider how each individual boy had developed personally with his emotional intelligence as well as his actual brainpower intelligence. All those sorts of things had to be studied as well.

What's his character? Is he introvert or extrovert, or is he just being a teenage boy?

We had to work in small groups and then take sessions individually. We had to go to different places to take the sessions, as well. I went to Cambuur, Zwolle and FC Twente. Every two or three weeks we had to go to games and write analytical reports about them. We had to analyse everything – the tactics of both teams, what happened on the pitch, what was the reaction of the one team to counteract the other team's tactics? To be honest, I was pretty good at that side of things, I do like the tactical side of the game. However, there are some coaches that are now professional coaches who weren't able to make it in this way. There are those I could name, but I'm not going to, who only got their Senior Licence because they were international players. They only had to do the Pro Licence, which is really quite easy. If you played a certain number of games for Holland, I think it was if you played 50 times, you could apply directly for the Pro Licence. So, these ones went from having nothing straight into having a Pro Licence; they could skip all the other levels. Really, everything that they needed they should have been taught when they were players, anyway. If you have a couple of brain cells it should be really easy.

When I gained my licence, I received an invitation to go over to Toronto in Canada. I stayed there for four weeks, during which time I met Paul Okumu, who had moved to Canada from his native Uganda and played in the Canadian Professional Soccer League. We did some training sessions together and a year later we went back for some more sessions. We did that three times. Back in Holland I gained some experience at a couple of amateur teams before training the under-19s at Emmen and then taking a position at FC Twente. When I was at Twente, Paul brought over some Canadian players for trials, some really good players. It was because of this and the good times that we'd had in Canada that, in 2015, Paul and I decided to set up a soccer experience. We called the company DutchCan Soccer. The name is an amalgamation of Dutch and Canadian and also has the inference that the Dutch can, we can provide good training sessions and teach you.

I set up the Theo ten Caat Academy, under the DutchCan umbrella, after seeing queues of young boys and girls at my amateur club who were just waiting around until they could get some training. We had a session on a Wednesday afternoon when anybody who was interested could come along, and over 100 kids turned up. There were four different sessions a year of six weeks each, and there were some really good players. After the initial start-up and seeing that there was some interest, we then had a couple of different age groups going, from 8 to 12 and then early teens. I did some individual one-on-one sessions as well with some youngsters, including Milan Smith, who is now playing at Cambuur – I trained him on Wednesday evenings for about a year.

The academy has actually grown really nicely. In 2022 we started the TTC Selection in which the most talented boys are invited to train once a week together, and we regularly have matches against clubs like Emmen and Groningen. There's also a girls' team that has recently been set up as well.

I've also been asked by one or two clubs to make a presentation about youth football and to take a session for them, including Aberdeen. Neil Simpson asked me to come over so I gave the Aberdeen coaches a presentation about the Dutch style of training and I also took the under-19 team of FC Twente over to play a couple of matches.

It's a lot of fun, but it's also a lot of hard work, too. It isn't just a case of waiting for the kids to come around to sign up for a session, there's lots of administration to do, social media, all that kind of thing. Having a football academy is really nice and you can see when players get better, which is very rewarding. I like to let the boys learn how to play the game naturally. Yes, of course I give them coaching and try to help them with their techniques and tell them what to do in certain situations on the pitch, but I always like it when they try to work out solutions for themselves, as well. When they're playing games I just let them play on. There are many coaches who will blow their whistle and stop the match and then explain why somebody could have passed a little bit earlier or why it probably wasn't a good idea to go on a dribble in a certain situation and things like that, before restarting the play again, but I like just letting them play and to work things out for themselves on the spur of the moment. Learning to think and react for yourself is an important thing in life anyway, not just in football. You have to learn from your mistakes. Outside of playing the games I'm always asking questions and opinions from the boys, but I like the action to continue. Off the pitch I'm always questioning, I try to never just tell them, I like them to try to work it out for themselves.

'What should you do in this situation? Do you think that thing happened?'

Then if another boy answers, I tell them, 'No, I'm not asking you, I'm asking him. I want to know *his* answer. Maybe your answer is right, but I want to know what *he* thinks.'

It trains them to think about things more, and not only before the game but during it as well. You need to make split-second decisions and I want to try to train their minds to be able to do that.

I also like to play the players in different positions. If I have a left full-back I like to sometimes play him in midfield or as a winger or move him across to be a centre-half. It helps them to develop an all-round game and also to appreciate what players in other positions might want from them as a full-back.

I also run a boot camp. This has nothing to do with football, it's more about getting people into shape. There are lots of people, more these days than when I was a youngster actually, that don't seem to be doing much in the way of physical exercise when they're younger, but when they hit 35 or 40 they see the need for a bit more fitness and want to start to train. I have a group of about 15 to 20 people who are coming every week and they're a really nice group. I like doing this, it's fun. Sometimes we do power sessions but mostly it's the general fitness things, squats, lunges, burpees, push-ups, those kinds of things, exercises for stomachs. I had a lady who was 45 when she started and she couldn't lift the bar up. Now she can do it great, up and over her head. That's what I like to see, people who want to try and improve. It's really nice to see them getting faster and stronger.

It's seeing the improvement in people that any coach or physical instructor wants. With my football coaching and my soccer schools, I know that not everybody will become a professional player but the main thing is that they enjoy what they're doing, take it seriously while having fun at the same time, do their very best, and if they can improve and go away thinking that Theo ten Caat is a good coach and a nice man, then I consider my job done.

November Rain – Why
I'll Always Be a Don

*If I was Aberdeen chairman, nobody with a
connection to Celtic or Rangers would be joining
the club, full stop.*

I COUNT myself as an Aberdeen supporter. I always look to
see how they get on and my wife and I speak about our time in
Scotland a lot. I'll always have an affinity with Aberdeen that
I don't have with my Dutch teams. I hope they win but if they
lose I don't get overly upset, and if they're playing in a good
game I hope the best team wins. With Aberdeen, though, it's a
completely different feeling.

In all honesty, I don't really know why this is. I've thought
about it a lot. I can only surmise that living in Aberdeen for
three years really helped form us as a family because we were
away from home and had to really make a go of it. We had lots
of visitors coming over from Holland all the time, but it wasn't
like when people would visit us before. Now they were going
over to a foreign country to visit us in our city, and it's a city
that's really in my system. We lived in Morningside Avenue,
about five miles from Pittodrie. I still remember seeing the

European games from 1983. I remember watching the matches against Bayern Munich live on television because we could get the German channels in Holland at the time.

Another factor, I think, was that Aberdeen were always fighting against Rangers and Celtic. Those two always looked down on us and we were so determined to beat them. Maybe that's another reason. I just don't have the same feeling with any other club that I do for Aberdeen, even FC Twente. They were my club when I was growing up, my dad supported them and used to take me along to the games, but I'm not really a supporter anymore. I hope they win but that's as far as it goes. I still can't abide Rangers. I never had a good feeling in Glasgow and I never had a good feeling in Edinburgh, but Aberdeen was home. It's funny that I just don't like the colour blue. When I'm coaching I always use red cones, never the blue ones. I never use the blue bibs. Red is the colour. Why? Because it's your heart. If I was the chairman of Aberdeen I would steer clear of appointing anyone from Celtic or Rangers. I know Alex Ferguson was a Rangers guy, but he was out to prove them wrong. He was blamed for their losing the 1969 Scottish Cup Final to Celtic and banished to the junior team. When he was manager at Pittodrie he was determined to beat them. Now, if I was Aberdeen chairman, nobody with a connection to Celtic or Rangers would be joining the club, full stop.

I've already spoken about the first time I played in an Aberdeen shirt in the tall ships game against Manchester United. It was that day when I really knew I had made the right choice in coming to Pittodrie. From that day on I was an Aberdeen supporter.

In Holland everything was organised, so organised. That doesn't mean there was no organisation in Scotland, of course, but in Holland we do everything the same. We have breakfast together, the pre-match meal together, everything is scheduled so the manager knows exactly what's going on. For that game against United, I, my wife and my son had breakfast at home and then we went for a walk in Duthie Park, a beautiful park a couple of miles away from the ground. That's what would normally happen in Holland, a walk after breakfast and then some sleep before the match preparations. And then before the game we didn't have a pre-match meal together, so we had to take that at home as well. After I had eaten – chicken and rice to give me a lot of carbs – I drove to Pittodrie and stopped by the harbour.

That was something I always used to do during my time there, I liked it by the harbour. It was where I used to go just to spend a few minutes to hone my concentration. Just as I got there on that day, the song 'November Rain' by Guns N' Roses came on the radio. 'November Rain' was my favourite song and it still is to this day. It just seemed one of those perfect moments. I've had a nice walk, had lunch with my wife and son, I'm off to play my first game for my new club in a new country against the famous Manchester United, and now they're playing my song for me. It just felt like everything was in the right place. 'November Rain' now also has that connection with my Aberdeen debut, and every time I hear that song my mind goes back to that day on 5 August 1991 and it makes me smile. I see the harbour in front of me.

When I arrived at Pittodrie, I parked my car in the gravel car park opposite the stadium and walked into the main entrance. You have the sign for Aberdeen Football Club, there are pictures on the walls, the doors to the boardroom and the manager's office, and the first place I always went to was the boot room. I can still smell the boots, that distinct aroma of clean, greased leather. I used to just sit there for a while because it was such a lovely place. I sat there for a few minutes and took my boots to the dressing room. All the lads arrived one by one and we had a bit of a team talk followed by a cup of coffee. I always have a coffee before a game – the British drink tea but I drink coffee – and started to get my kit on. When getting dressed for a match, I always put my left sock on first, then my right sock, then my left boot and then my right boot. Every time. That's standard. I do that before I put my shirt and shorts on. Every player has their funny little thing and that's mine. I also always play with long sleeves, but that evening it was warm and everybody else had short sleeves, so I had to ask for a shirt with long sleeves. I always like to play with my arms covered, even in 30 degrees. I don't know why, but I hate playing in short sleeves because I feel naked. It feels to me like I'm on the beach enjoying the sunshine rather than being fully prepared to do a job on the pitch. It's a mental thing. Then when I'm ready I just sit down and don't move from my spot until we go out on to the pitch. Some players like to go into the shower room to kick a ball against the wall, some like to chat and tell jokes, but I like to sit quietly and tune my mind in.

When we got out on to the pitch there were pipers playing, and I can still hear them now. They were still playing during our warm-up. We were all out there getting ready, doing a bit of running and passing before going back into the dressing room for the last words from the manager before coming out to start the game. Before going back inside I always liked to do a couple of runs without the ball and always ended with some long passes. I would grab one of the other players and we would pass 30, 40, 50 yards to each other. The match finished in a 1-1 draw, although they beat us on penalties, and to top off a perfect day I scored a nice goal from 20 yards and my Aberdeen career was underway.

Back in the dressing room afterwards I would go through the same ritual, only in reverse. Shirt off first, then shorts, right boot, left boot, right sock and finally left sock. Then the young boys came in, the reserves, and that was a surprise for me as well. In Holland everybody took care of their own kit but there they were taking my boots to the boot room to clean them for me. Not only that but, when everybody had showered and was ready to leave, they came back in with the vacuum cleaners to hoover out the dressing room. I was wondering what was going on but it was just something else I had to get used to.

Another thing, of course, was my name. How the newspaper headline writers had some fun with that! Ten Caat still has nine lives, Caat's whiskers, Top Caat, etc. In fact, when my wife and I first arrived in Aberdeen there were some supporters at the airport who recognised me. How, I don't know, but they were saying, 'There he is, the Top Caat.'

When I signed I had to do a press conference, which was actually the first one I had ever given. There were a lot of journalists present, newspapers, television and radio. I didn't know I would have to do it until that morning when my agent, Ton van Dalen, said that we had to be at Pittodrie at this particular time. I had no idea what to expect so I read the newspapers just to prepare myself a bit. When it started I just said that I was very pleased to be there, Aberdeen is a big club and to play for them gives me a better chance of getting in the Dutch national team, all the usual things that they want to hear. To be honest, I didn't really understand what half of them were saying!

My not understanding the Scottish language fluently was a bit of a feature in those early days. There was a dinner that I went to with my wife, along with Ton van Dalen, with the Aberdeen board members and coaches. Throughout the evening my wife was looking at me all the time.

'What are they saying?' she was asking. 'Is this English?'

'I don't know,' I said to her, 'it doesn't sound like the English I learned at school.'

They gave us a menu of things that we could choose to eat and I said to Ton van Dalen that he could choose for us because I didn't know what most of the things were.

'We'll get salmon,' he said. 'Salmon is always safe.'

Then we had to choose dessert. The dessert menu came and I was looking at it with my wife, but all the desserts had fancy names that I had never heard of before. We just didn't understand what was on it. I asked for a fruit basket, not knowing what it was. It sounded good, it sounded healthy, a pretty safe choice. Plus, I'm making a good impression here choosing the healthy option. When it came, it was a basket with an apple and a banana inside. Everybody else was having their fancy desserts and nice little cakes and beautiful-looking ice creams, and my wife and I were sharing an apple and a banana! The thing is, after a couple of months of living there we realised the food on offer in Aberdeen is beautiful. Aside from the local stuff, the Chinese and Indian restaurants there are really nice. Here we were, though, after about six hours in the country, not having a clue, then going to the nice fancy dinner and having an apple and a banana!

There was another occasion, half social, half work, where an Aberdeen legend almost made me an alcoholic. The legend in question was Willie Miller. I've spoken here about my relationship with Willie in a player and coach scenario, but I have to say as a man, away from that environment, I have absolutely no problem with him whatsoever. Before Willie became the manager, when Alex Smith was still in charge, he and I, along with our wives, attended a bit of a soiree at one of the supporters' clubs. It was the first time that I went to one of these evenings and I didn't know what to expect. So we were sitting around a table, there was a game of bingo going on, and somehow the conversation turns to whisky. I didn't know that Scotland was famous for whisky and I was saying to Willie that it would be interesting to visit a distillery to see how they make it. He was drinking Drambuie that evening and he asked if I wanted to try some. I said I was happy drinking my cola. Before this we had had a few nights out with the boys, but I had never drunk alcohol. I don't like the taste of beer and that's what the other players were drinking. I would normally just have a Coca-Cola. It was the same in Holland whenever I went out with the team, I never touched alcohol. Willie, however, resorted to a good line of persuasion.

'You do realise what you have to do later, don't you?' he asked.

'What do you mean?'

'Well, there will be some dancing and we will have to participate.'

'But Willie,' I said, 'I'm not a dancer. I'm the guy who stands in the corner watching the other people dance.'

He was insistent. 'No, no, no, there will be dancing and we have to do it. There will be some quite strange dances, as well, and you also have to give a speech.'

'Well, you can do the speech,' I said, 'you're the Aberdeen legend. I'm just the new guy.'

'No, Theo, you have to do the speech, I've done enough in my time.'

It was at that point I said to Willie, 'Okay, I'll try a Drambuie.'

He had made me nervous! A bottle of Drambuie arrived on the table and Willie and I were drinking it together. My first taste I thought was a bit strong so he suggested I put some coke in it, so my next one was Drambuie and coke. There was less and less coke going into the subsequent shots, and when it was time for dancing the four of us were up. I remember we had to do some local dance where we had to do some quite strange things that I had never seen before on a dance floor. By the end of the night, fuelled by Drambuie, I then had to give my speech. I have no idea what I actually said, but I did it. That evening is the reason why I now drink whisky.

* * *

In all of our conversations, Theo was eloquent, charming, funny and always had plenty to say. Therefore, one of my favourite moments in all the time that we spent talking was when I asked him about his routine of getting ready for a game.

'What would happen if you didn't put your left sock on first?' I asked.

This was honestly the only time he was ever lost for words. He was genuinely stumped. He thought about it for a few seconds then looked at me as if I was completely mad.

'Impossible,' was his answer, 'that would never happen. If you want to drive your car you have to start your engine. It's impossible to do anything without it. That would never happen. Impossible situation. Don't ask me such a silly thing ...'

My Dream Team

EVERY FOOTBALL supporter's favourite pastime is picking fantasy teams. I'm fortunate enough to have played with many great players, and here's my dream team made up of players that I've played with. When I say that I've played with many great players, I mean great in various ways. Some were obviously brilliant players who excited the crowd whenever they got on the ball, while some were great team players who got through a lot of work, much of it unnoticed by the public but very much appreciated by their team-mates. Choosing a dream team isn't always as easy as it seems. You need balance and you need a mixture of different types of players. Having a team full of flair players won't work because you need someone to put their foot in and get everyone else going through the difficult times. Having said that, looking through my team, it would be lovely to watch and has proper footballers from back to front. After all, it *is* a dream team and I was a flair player and I can pick who I want!

Theo Snelders

I played with Theo for three years at FC Twente when I started out in my career and it was brilliant to team up with him again at Aberdeen. When I first went over to Scotland he helped me out a lot. He's a good guy.

What I noticed throughout all the years I played professional football is that goalies are, and please excuse me for the word, but they're lunatics! They're part of the team but also not part of the team. They live in their own world. If you're a player out on the pitch and your team-mate makes a mistake you try to help him out, there are ten of you working together. The goalies are a lot more individual and they only have their back four to organise. Now that I'm a coach I tell my goalkeepers that their job is not to make saves, and that if they have to make saves they've done something wrong because then they didn't organise their back four properly. Of course, the defence can't win everything all the time, so obviously the goalie has to make saves, but your first job as a goalkeeper is to try to get your defence to avoid giving the opposition chances. That's what Theo was brilliant at. He was always busy talking to his defenders, shouting at them, pulling them into position. If he hadn't been such a good organiser he would have been twice as busy in every game.

Aside from his organisational skills, I think that of all the goalkeepers I ever played with Theo was the best in one against one situations because he's a monster. If you go into a one against one with Theo the best thing for you to do is to run away from the ball and let him have it. 'I'm not going up against you, otherwise I might end up in the hospital.' Even in training he went 100 per cent for the ball, and if he took the man out as well then he didn't care. He just loved going for the ball – high balls, low balls, he would just fling himself at them. He had some injuries because of that. I can remember at FC Twente on the training ground he went for one ball against his team-mate and had his tongue cut in two. It just opened up and all the blood was coming out. But that's how Theo was, he was 100 per cent all the time. He was very professional, he would go to the gym and he would always take his little arm weights with him wherever he went. At Aberdeen I was his room-mate for a while for away games and I would be trying to sleep but he would be playing with his weights. He was always totally focused on his football. A brilliant goalkeeper.

Stewart McKimmie

A great footballer and a great guy. Every opponent in a one against one situation against Stewart McKimmie will find himself in difficulties. He was fast, he had a great tackle and he could play football as well. You don't win 40 caps for Scotland for nothing. He actually scored the winning goal for Scotland against Argentina in a friendly game when Argentina were the world champions. He was a fighter, he was a winner and he was a proper football player.

Stewart knew exactly what he could do, so he never did strange things. He knew what his talents were and that's probably the most important thing for a football player. If you don't know what you shouldn't do, that's when it all goes wrong. Stewart knew what his strengths were and always played to them. He always worked really hard in training sessions, a really good colleague to have in the team. If I was the manager of this team, I could give him a task and I know he would do it. He was always focused on what the manager told him to do. He never gave up and was a very positive guy.

He was one of my favourite players and one of my favourite people, as well. He came into the Aberdeen squad under Alex Ferguson and survived a succession of managers with nobody wanting to replace him. He played under Ferguson, Ian Porterfield, Alex Smith, Willie Miller and Roy Aitken, which proves what a good player he was. Normally a manager will come in and he will have his own ideas of how he wants to play and have in mind players he wants to bring in to play for him, but none of these replaced Stewart. They all knew that he could do a job for them. That also shows what a great player he was.

I think in a way it's a shame he never tried to go to play in Europe. Maybe he never had the chance but it would have been interesting to see him playing with a top team abroad. He certainly would have had that quality but he stayed with Aberdeen because he loved playing for the club, and fair play to him for that. He really was top quality and I think to this day he's still underrated, even though he won many trophies with Aberdeen and gained so many international caps for Scotland.

Nico-Jan Hoogma

I played with Nico at FC Twente. He came to Twente from Cambuur and when he left he went to Germany to play for

Hamburg. He was very strong in the air, a typical Dutch defender. Nico-Jan was a great organiser. He knew he wasn't that fast so he was really good at organising the defence and keeping the team in a good shape. He was strong and good in the challenge, and offensively he scored a lot of goals with his head so he was very useful at corners and set pieces. He was a really good old-fashioned defender. His passing wasn't his greatest asset but, like Stewart McKimmie, he knew what he was good at and what he could do, so didn't try to do anything more. He would have the ball and play it out to the first player who was standing free and begin the build-up like that. And that's fair enough because a defender's job is to make sure you don't concede.

There's a tendency for people to say, 'Five-four, what a brilliant game that was.' That might be a nice game to watch but it was a terrible game for the managers. If it was 5-4 then too many mistakes were made. A 1-0 or 0-0 is probably a better game tactically and organisationally, and that's what Nico-Jan was so good at, organising his colleagues. He was such a solid defender, very reliable.

When he left FC Twente he went to Hamburg for a few years before coming back to Holland to play the last couple of years at Heracles. He became managing director at Heracles and also went to the Dutch football association, the KNVB, to be the technical director, so that's an indication of how well he could read a game and how organised he was. He's now back at Heracles as technical director.

Alex McLeish

I really don't have to explain why I've included Alex McLeish. Aside from being brilliant, he's one of the nicest people I've ever met in football. He gave me a hard time sometimes but I guess I deserved it. He knew that hard words sometimes do better than soft words. On the other hand, he was also very kind to me off the field. We lived close to each other and he was always helpful.

The only mistake he ever made was becoming the manager of Glasgow Rangers. I mean, I have my boundaries. I can't fathom why an Aberdeen man, and such a legend at that, would go to Rangers or Celtic. I was a Dutch guy playing for Aberdeen and I hated Rangers and Celtic! I hated Hearts and Hibs. I hated Dundee United. That's the way Aberdeen gets you, they're your club. I never felt this way in Holland against any of our rivals, they were just opponents. I never had that feeling inside me towards other clubs that I did when I played for Aberdeen. So, no, I wouldn't have gone to Rangers, but that was Alex's choice.

Aside from that he was wonderful. He always took care of me, he gave me advice and was always there for me. He was a real captain. He was the leader of the pack. Everybody listened to Alex. In the game he was obviously a really good player and going for challenges was hard, but I can't remember him making many fouls. I've never seen him deliberately go and hurt somebody. His challenges, most of which he won, were hard but fair and he played simply, as well. He deserves to be in my dream team, it would be an injustice if he wasn't. I never played with Willie Miller, otherwise I would have picked him as well for the McLeish–Miller partnership. When I played with Alex he was the glue that held the team together. He's the captain of my team, the only choice. Alex is top class. One of the best players I ever played with and, in combination with his other qualities, a top guy as well. He's probably the most important player in this team.

Rob McKinnon

I played with Rob at FC Twente. In the pre-season, Hans Meyer, who was the manager at Twente, came to me and asked me if I knew this left full-back who played for Motherwell because he had signed him. I did remember him. He was technically good and liked to get up and down the pitch, not just staying back in defence. I played directly in front of him on the left-hand side and defensively he helped me a lot because he was another one who liked to keep it simple. The way we played at Twente was that I linked up a lot with our left-winger, so when our opponents broke out often there were people running past me and I was sometimes in a two against one situation in midfield. Rob would push forward to help me out. He wasn't particularly fast but tactically he was very good, he was fast in his mind. If you're fast in your mind you don't necessarily have to be very quick because you can see what the best solution would be anyway.

My relationship with Rob off the pitch also makes a difference as to why he's selected in this team, and he should be grateful for that!

Jan Sørensen

Jan was a Danish player who played a few times for their national team. He played in Belgium for FC Brugge, who were a top team at the time. They were the champions of Belgium and also did well in Europe. We were quite similar in the way we played. We were both attacking midfield players who liked to pass the ball and tried to get into the box. The difference was that I was more of a passer and he was more of a runner with the ball. He had a tremendous quality in that he could speed up when he was sprinting. He would be running with the ball and, just when his opponent thought he had it, he would speed up and get away. He could also score goals.

He was a father figure for me when I joined Twente in 1984. I was only a young boy at the time and Jan was about 30, and he was the top man at the club, the best player. He's probably one of the best players that ever played for FC Twente. I was still going to school at the time, so I was always late for afternoon training. The training sessions began at 2.00 but my classes didn't finish until 2.10. I took my bike to the stadium, got into my training gear, took my bike and ran across the stadium to where the boys were training and threw my bike into the bushes. The other players had already had their warm-up by then, whereas my warm-up was frantically pedalling my bike! That's how it went with me for the first two years.

In the school holidays I was able to come in for training in the morning as well. So, one particular morning, we were sitting down on the old wooden benches we used to have, waiting for training to begin, but the kit didn't come. Jan said to me, 'Theo, will you go inside and bring out the kit so we can start training?'

Me being 19, I said to him, 'Jan, that's not my job, somebody else has to do that.'

He stood up and sat himself down next to me. He put his arm around my shoulder and whispered in my ear so nobody else could hear, 'Theo, I give you ten seconds – no, five. If you don't do as I say and get the stuff we need to start training, you will last five minutes on the field and then you will wake up in the hospital.'

I immediately stood up and went to the dressing room and walked back and forth three times to make sure we had all the kit to start the session. Jan just said, very calmly, 'Thank you very much, Theo, thank you for listening to me.'

I didn't really know the rules when I first started out. When we had lunch together or a pre-match meal, I was always talking at the dining table, giving my opinion. Jan let me do it for a couple of weeks and then he rose from his chair, walked around the table and came to me. He put his hands on my shoulders and he said to me, 'I've noticed that you like to talk, and there's nothing wrong with that, but I want you now to be quiet every time we have a meal together. If it's breakfast, lunch or dinner, whenever this team is having a meal together you be quiet until we've all finished, until the moment you get into the team and, because of you, we're winning games and you start making money for us.'

It took me three months to get into the first team. The season started in July and I made my debut in October, but I still didn't say anything. As the season went on, I was in the team and we were winning games but I was still quiet at the table. After a while, Jan stood up again and walked round the tables towards me and stood in exactly the same position with his hands on my shoulders and said, 'Theo, now you're a member of the team and we're winning games, I allow you now – no, I demand you now – to speak if you have an opinion at the table.'

It still took me a further three weeks to open my mouth!

Unfortunately, I only played one year with Jan because then he went to Feyenoord and also on to Ajax. When he was at Ajax he had an argument with Johan Cruyff. One day Cruyff came into the dressing room and gave his opinion on how to play the game and Jan stood up and said, 'You're talking rubbish. We have to do this, then we do that, and then the problem is solved. What you're saying is totally nuts. You're a nutter.' He said that to Johan Cruyff!

The thing is, Jan was a top player as well, full of confidence and belief in himself. To get to the very top you absolutely have to do that. What he said to Cruyff, it wasn't just for show or effect. If he believed somebody was wrong – anybody, the coach, Johan Cruyff, anybody – he would say so. You have to be confident. If you're not confident in yourself how can you convince other people?

His skills in midfield earn him a place. Plus, I'm also scared not to have him in my team ...!

Jim Bett

I always had a good connection with Jim on the pitch and off the pitch as well. We spent some time together playing golf, which was nice. Once every two or three weeks we would have a round of golf and some lunch and talk about anything and everything. Jim found himself in a similar situation to me in that he fell out of favour with Willie Miller, but if you look at his career – playing in Iceland, playing for Aberdeen, playing for Rangers and playing for Lokeren in Belgium, as well as in the Scotland international team – he was a great footballer. He was adaptable, too. He could play European style and Scottish style. He was able to run forward and score goals, he was a good passer and his reading of the game was brilliant. He could do anything and had the respect of all the players.

He's one of those players that pulls things together on the pitch. When he plays well the team plays well. He was also a really good guy to have in the dressing room, and that's important. What happens in the dressing room is almost as important as what happens on the pitch. If a dressing room is good, if it's happy and everyone gets along well with each other, then you play good games. On the other hand, if the dressing room is not that good you need people in there who will help you out. If the manager comes in and gives you a hard time then you have to have players in there who will talk to you and give you confidence again. Jim Bett was one of those players.

To put it simply, Jim was one of the best midfield players I've ever played with. He's a brilliant guy, he was world-class.

He made over 300 appearances for Aberdeen and in my opinion is one of their best-ever players.

Phillip Cocu

I played with Phillip at Vitesse. He was a young guy at that time. He joined us from AZ Alkmaar. I saw him do things when he was 22, 23 that I didn't even know were possible. He was so good and so talented. His passing was great, he could score goals and was really good when attacking players. As you grow older you tend to develop a style but back then he was so young and so fresh and free in his mind. Anything he thought about doing, he just went and did it. Just look at his career – Vitesse to PSV, PSV to Barcelona and 100 international appearances. Everybody who knows football knows the talent of Phillip Cocu.

I do think, though, as a manager he's a little bit too soft. He was in charge of PSV and went over to England with Derby County, and now he's back at Vitesse. I look at him now and can't help feeling that somewhere along the line he has lost a bit of confidence.

As a player, though, he was great, he did brilliantly, an absolutely top player.

Milko Djurovski

I played with Milko at Groningen. He was the second striker and I played behind him. He was a magician. When he was on the ball his dribbling was phenomenal, he moved with such pace. We actually played against him at Groningen in Europe when he was at Partizan Belgrade and his goals knocked us out of the competition. Actually, before we played Belgrade, in the previous round they beat Celtic in a crazy tie. In the second leg Darius Dziekanowski scored four for Celtic and they still ended up going out. That game finished 5-4 and it was 6-6 on aggregate, so Belgrade went through on the away goals rule. Milko got his transfer to Groningen because of the impact he had made in Europe that season and not least for the part he played in knocking us out!

When I had the ball I would always look for Milko, we had a good combination. He scored a lot of goals, was a bit of an individual and is still a cult hero at Groningen. There's a radio station called Milko Radio that reports on what's going on at Groningen. It shows you what an impact he made when he was at the club because he was only there for two seasons.

John Bosman

Started out at Ajax, moved to Anderlecht in Belgium and then he came and played for a couple of years at Twente. Considering I played in Scotland where there were many great headers of the ball, I've never seen a guy who was so good at heading the ball on target. Even if he was standing ten yards in front of the near post, he had such good technique with his head that he could score from angles that most players couldn't even do with their foot.

He had a good career at international level, as well. He didn't win so many caps because he was playing at the time of Marco van Basten and Ruud Gullit, but he was part of the

European Championship-winning squad in 1988. He was such a good target man.

Roy Makaay

He was a youngster at Vitesse, there at the same time as Phillip Cocu. Even at that time you could see he was a brilliant finisher and would go on to be a star. He wasn't really that technical but in the box he was lethal. When I met him he was a teenager and already a good player. He came into the team really quickly. He scored his goals and as he got older he kept developing himself. When he left Holland he played in Spain with Deportivo La Coruña and then went to Germany with Bayern Munich and really showed everybody how good he was.

Makaay was special because, actually, his technique wasn't the best. If you compare him to the other top Dutch strikers of that time – players like Dennis Bergkamp or Ruud van Nistelrooy – they were technically a lot better, but in front of goal he was superb. Give him the ball and it's a fair chance he would score. Roy Makaay was one of the best finishers I've seen. He was always there on the spot, in the right place, scoring goals.

* * *

So that's the dream team that I've played with. If they were all together in their prime I have no doubt they would have a good shot at winning the Champions League. Three Scottish defenders! I mean, if you can resist being conquered by the Roman army, then you can defend on a football pitch!

Afterword – What They Said About Him

THEO TEN Caat clearly had a varied, at times bizarre, but thoroughly enjoyable career as a professional footballer. He speaks of his former team-mates with affection, but what did they really think of him? I contacted a few of his peers and asked them for their honest comments and opinions on not only Theo the player but Theo the man as well. Below are their responses, in their own words ...

Billy Ashcroft

Team-mate at FC Twente

The reason I went over to play football in Holland was because, when I was at Middlesbrough, we signed a Dutchman called Heini Otto. He was an attacking midfielder who had joined us from Twente. He had such a good touch and had clearly been taught how to play properly. He's still spoken of as a legend among the Middlesbrough supporters. Having played with him in England, I thought that it would be an experience to go the other way, so I signed for his former club. That's where I met Theo. He was just starting out then but I knew what he would be like as a footballer from his personality. He was a smashing kid, a great talker, who fitted in really well right from the beginning. Even though he was still young and right at the start of his career, he wasn't shy but really confident.

One of the big differences over in Holland at the time was in the way the kids were trained. The pitches were smaller, they were taught and encouraged to learn their skills and to just have a good time on the pitch. They were taught that football should be enjoyable and I completely agree with that. In England back then, kids of six or seven were playing on full-sized pitches, which was no good for them. When Theo made the breakthrough at Twente it was obvious that he knew exactly how football should be played. The younger lads weren't particularly interested in tactics and, even when the coach was talking in training, half of the players, Theo included, just couldn't stand still. They would have a ball and be touching it all the time, left foot to right foot. It was a real eye-opener for me but it helped make them as skilful as they were, and Theo was a very skilful player. He always played with a smile on his face and, me being a centre-forward, I was pleased to have another attacking wide player in the squad who I knew would feed me quality crosses.

In all honesty, I didn't see a lot of Theo when he came over to Aberdeen because by that time I had finished my career at Tranmere Rovers and got myself an Everton season ticket, so I spent my Saturdays at Goodison Park. Had Theo come down to England to play, I'm sure he would have been a big hit. He liked to play off the cuff, whereas at Aberdeen Willie Miller seemed to prefer playing in the more traditional British way.

Theo is a great lad. I catch up with him occasionally on social media, and it was my pleasure to be his team-mate, if only for a short time.

Eric Groeleken

Team-mate at FC Twente and Groningen

Theo could bring a big advantage to any team with his brilliant left foot. He also had good stamina and could run and run – he was like a horse! As a person he was a lovely guy to talk to and to work with and we often had a good laugh together. He had strong opinions and confidence in himself and his ability, which is something else I liked about him, maybe because we're similar in this way. We got on very well.

Gordon Hill

Team-mate at FC Twente

Theo was a young player just breaking through in Dutch football when I played with him. He had a lot of talent and would give his all for the team. That, actually, was sometimes his problem. He was also studying at the time so was having to fit in both studying and playing, and he wanted to do it all. I liked playing with Theo because he was always willing to learn and ask questions. I would have recommended him to any English clubs looking for a young player with ability.

Theo was in his learning stages of the professional game. If he had gone to a top club then of course he could have been selected for his country.

Scottish football is very different to Dutch football and had he been signed by Nottingham Forest it would have alerted the selectors from the Dutch FA. Brian Clough would have given him a chance and he may have done well. We will never know.

Nico-Jan Hoogma

Team-mate at FC Twente

I met Theo towards the end of his career and I liked the kind of player he was. He was one of the creative members of our squad, the type of player I've always admired. I always liked, and still like, the ones who can get the ball and do something with it. I played as a defender and knew that if I gave the ball to Theo he wouldn't waste it. I could trust him to move it on or play a good pass or dribble. Also, he was a very intelligent player who wouldn't just hit it forward to start an attack. He would make sure that he gave it to a team-mate and not just create a 50-50.

Away from football he was also a very good artist, his paintings are brilliant. A lot of the time when a person is artistic you can see it in many different things, not just one, and Theo had that artistry in him. He was artistic in his fingers and you could see that in his play as well.

Brian Irvine

Team-mate at Aberdeen

I really enjoyed playing with the Dutch guys, they were very focused and I like that about the Dutch mentality. Theo is a wonderful human being and I'm thankful to know him.

Martin Koopman

Team-mate at FC Twente and coach at Veendam

Theo joined FC Twente a couple of years after I moved there from Go Ahead Eagles. He was a young player just starting out in his football career but he didn't seem like a young boy and always acted in a mature way. Sometimes it would seem like Theo wasn't paying much attention but he was an observer and everything that was happening he was recording in his mind.

When he came in, we immediately had a good bond because we shared a sense of humour and he knew his place at the club, there was no pretension. On the pitch he had a great drive and kept going for 90 minutes. His insight into the game was excellent and he could read the game well. He could also philosophise like no other!

When he moved to Scotland, he fulfilled his tasks in the team in his own way. He was different to the other players and that's why there were some trainers who weren't big fans of Theo as a player. He could be stubborn in the way he wanted to play and had a different personality from the average players, but that made him stand out in a positive way, too.

I didn't expect Theo to become a coach because sometimes he could appear a bit dreamy, but he was able to put a lot of things into perspective. However, because he could analyse things well, that has enabled him to become a super coach.

In summary, Theo is a nice guy who you can learn a lot from as a player and he also has integrity.

Lee Richardson

Team-mate at Aberdeen

Theo ten Caat was a mad cat or, at least, an eccentric one! I think – in fact I know – that he would probably say the same thing about me.

Theo was a very skilful left-footed player who was technically very good. He probably didn't quite suit the physicality of Scottish football or, perhaps more accurately, Scottish football didn't suit him. He was always a purist and wanted to play the game in a certain way, which wasn't necessarily the vogue in Scotland at the time. He spent much of his time out wide on the left, although he probably wanted to play more centrally. Given his attributes, I believe that would have been his best position. He made up for a lack of pace with a nice left foot and a good ability to pass the ball both long and short.

I always remember his crazy sense of humour and his Joker-style laugh. He was a bit of a rebel, again like me. I think we bonded well as we were both outsiders to an extent – a crazy Dutch rebel and an Englishman playing in Scotland. We both wore our hair long and liked rock music. Theo was a good guy.

Scott Thompson

Team-mate at Aberdeen

I only crossed over with Theo for a couple of seasons. He was a great player and a great lad also.